America Lost?

What We Learned by Living in Mexico

Al and Biljana
Feinstein

PublishAmerica
Baltimore

First printing

PublishAmerica has allowed this work to remain exactly as the author intended, verbatim, without editorial input.

Hardcover 978-1-4489-3128-6
Softcover 978-1-4489-4955-7
PUBLISHED BY PUBLISHAMERICA, LLLP
www.publishamerica.com
Baltimore

Printed in the United States of America

This book is dedicated to my parents, Philip and Beatrice, and to my wife, Biljana, who all immigrated to America with the idea of becoming and living their lives as true and complete Americans.
It is also dedicated to all of the immigrants, before and after, with the same ideal.

"I just love America!" Philip would say.
"Don't you love America?" Biljana would say.

"Coming together is a beginning; keeping together is progress; working together is success." Henry Ford.

PREFACE

We all know and love the fact that America is the land of opportunity and the land of the free. We can feel that America is, and always has been, a sort of paradise for human rights and dignity due to the freedom and security for which America stands. At this point in time, however, could it be fair to say that our place in the world community has been damaged? Could we say that we have lost some of that sense of paradise?

This book is specifically designed to not always be politically correct. In fact, it is purposely designed to be apolitical.

The authors wish to only voice opinions and concerns as to why they believe America is not as well represented in today's time as they believe it has been in earlier years.

Some of the incidents, stories and anecdotes concerning individuals are not necessarily intended to describe particular persons. The stories are based on facts and incidents as the authors remembered them, but the names, locations and occupations may have changed.

All of the instances noted are not intended to single out Mexico. They are simply events, recollections and circumstances that occurred to the authors through their singular experience of living in Mexico combined with their visits and travels to other countries. They are written so as to amplify the basis of this book, which is to investigate and ask the questions, "Why do people denigrate America and Americans? How can we make Americans become more aware of what is actually happening today and to work to preserve that for which America stands?"

Research for this endeavor includes The Internet, Wikipedia Encyclopedia, local and other newspapers, Merriam-Webster Dictionary, biographies and books about the Founding Fathers and various other book and articles by well known and unknown writers.

Al and Biljana moved back to their home in Colorado after living in Mexico for three years. They continue to stay in contact with their friends and acquired families in Mexico.

The book is presented in a conversational style. The personal dialogue between Al and Biljana is the basis of the information and opinions offered. The discussion between the writers and the reader suggests that the reader can interact with the information and opinions.

"The budget should be balanced, the treasury should be filled, public debt should be reduced, the arrogance of officialdom should be tempered and controlled, and the assistance to foreign lands should be curtailed, lest Rome become bankrupt. People must again learn to work instead of living on public assistance." Cicero 55 B.C.

Contents

1
OBSERVATION AND REVELATION

"So, here I am, Al, sitting under a palapa, but sometimes laying on a towel and sometimes lounging in a beach chair, on the white soft sand beach of the Caribbean Sea in the City of Playa del Carmen, in the State of Quintana Roo in Mexico. I am looking out at the seven wonderful colors of brilliant blue and aqua ocean, as the Mayans describe it, watching seabirds do their natural things with the water and with me feeling the nice warming breeze on my body. I am living here fulltime, only after having lived my life as a working stiff up until now."

"As I sit and let my mind wander, for some unknown reason, I ask a question—How was I able to get here? I mean, what a question! What in the world made me ask this? Why now? So, I meditate on it, ponder it and try to work my mind in some sort of chronological order to see if I can reconstruct this personal phenomenon. Wow! What a job I have created for myself! I mean, come on, how can I do that? After all, I am now 73 years old and have no logical necessity to do such a thing. But, as it turns out, this idea is not mine alone. Now that I think of it, my wife, Biljana, came up with the idea after we had one of our philosophical talks while enjoying the warm weather on our balcony one evening not long ago."

Al and Biljana had been living in Mexico for about three years and made friends and acquaintances on a regular basis. The beauty of living in the growing city of Playa del Carmen is that it is not being populated by any particular group or nationality, which is not very different from the way many areas of America is being populated. It is an international community that attracts all types of people from all locations to invest, to settle, to visit, to enjoy, to make a home. Mexicans, Israelis, Italians, Canadians, Germans, Greeks, Dutch, Venezuelans, Colombians, Brazilians, Russians, Belizeans, Cape Verdens, Australians, Guatemalans, Yemenis and of course, Americans from around the country. What fun!

Because of this happy situation, Al and Biljana had the fortunate circumstance to talk with a variety of people and get many opinions and comments about many subjects. A particular subject that stood out dealt with America and Americans, specifically as it relates to the present situation around the world; the negative and unflattering things that were being said about America. It was not only non-Americans that were saying these things about America, Americans were saying them also!

Al and Biljana couldn't believe it and talked about this to each other on a continuing basis.

"So, what does this have to do with me sitting under this palapa at this time?" Al asks himself. "Well, it is exactly because I am sitting here that this comes to mind. The answer to my own question is—I am able to be here BECAUSE I am an American! The opportunities in my country and the circumstances of my life allowed me to dream of and actually arrive at this place at this time."

Although Al knows that other people from other countries are capable of the same thing, to him it remains a wonder that he has actually done it, and he knows that in America, anyone who has the desire can have it.

Thus, the experiences Al and Biljana had in their new environment were simply a reflection of the situation surrounding their time in Mexico. They had come to love this part of Mexico and the friends they made over the years. This environment offered beautiful beaches, wonderful weather (although very hot in August and September), fabulous sea, great foliage, different activities, exciting new adventures, a chance to become acquainted with people from many parts of the world and a new culture to absorb. And more! What fun! How exciting!

2
PERSONAL HISTORY

Al's family history is similar to Biljana's history, only a different time period. They both basically came from somewhere else. Europe. He was born in New York to immigrant Russian parents; she came here as an immigrant, from Yugoslavia. His parents, Pinchus (Philip) and Blume (Beatrice), came to America and became American citizens because of the opportunities afforded them, as was true with anybody else who wished to remove themselves from the oppression of the aftermath of the Russian revolution and Tsarist Russia as well as elsewhere in the world. The year was 1916. Biljana came to America to become an American citizen because of her desire to use her talents as she desired. And, being an intelligent woman, she had determined that America offered the best of prospects. The year was 1968.

After Biljana arrived in America, the first thing she noticed was the patriotism and love that Americans have for their Country. She consequently happily adapted this feeling of love for America for herself and has never looked back.

The 2008 Merriam-Webster Online Dictionary defines patriotism as "a love for or devotion to one's country." The 2007 Online Wikipedia Dictionary defines patriotism as "love of and/or devotion to one's country," and it adds "individual responsibility to fellow citizens is an inherent component of patriotism." Pride is defined as "a reasonable or justifiable self respect."

John H. Schaar, political theorist and Professor Emeritus at the University of California, Santa Cruz, states "To be a patriot is to have a patrimony; or, perhaps more accurately, the patriot is one who is grateful for a legacy and recognizes that the legacy makes him a debtor.... The gift of land, people, language, gods, memories, and customs, which is the patrimony of the patriot, defines what he or she is...The conscious patriot is one who feels deeply indebted for these gifts, grateful to the people and places through which they come, and determined to defend the legacy against enemies and pass it unspoiled to those who come after." (1).

The 2008 Merriam-Webster Online Dictionary defines patrimony as "an estate inherited from one's father or ancestor."

Although Biljana and Al only met in 1988, their desires, experience, concept of the good life, dreams and wishes were similar even prior to their meeting. They were not afraid to work, not afraid to take on unknowns, not afraid to be proud of themselves, not afraid to be proud Americans. Very important qualities, they believed. And, a tenet to which they thought most Americans subscribed.

Being aware of her situation and more than willing to be completely successful in her life, Biljana wanted her children and descendents to grow up in America, to be Americans and to be proud of it as she is.

Al had once read an anonymous statement in a magazine article that said "you can't change your mind about loving your country because of the current government" (*in power*). Emphasis author.

At the WindsOfChange.net website, there is a statement by an unknown (to this author) writer that says "Successful societies are ones in which each member adds to the social capital that can be passed on to the next generation. To do that—save, rather than spend, to build rather than consume—requires some sense of obligation, of one's place in a chain that stretches from your ancestors to your descendents—and which is broad enough to expand 'ancestor' and 'descendent' to include other than your blood kin."

3
LEARNING TIME

The many times Al and Biljana talked about this state of affairs while sitting and sunning on the beach just about every day, the more they discovered things about themselves. One was that they were in constant awe about how negatively people in Mexico, including those natural born Americans and naturalized Americans living in or visiting Mexico, were talking about America and Americans at this point in time. They also heard disparaging remarks about the President of the United States (most often the individual, not the office).

"Now," Al says to Biljana, "as with all citizens, it is perfectly acceptable to disagree with the President. His policies and methods of governing are, as is a constitutional right in America, up to scrutiny, private and public. However, the Office of the President needs to be at the highest level of pride and respect. After all, he is the head of the most powerful country in the world and the leader of the free world."

We Americans get to choose who our President will be.

And, Biljana says while getting a darker tan on the beach, "Thank God we have a governmental system that has sets of checks and balances built into it so that our leaders can be changed, both by necessity and by time." Someone once said that the genius of democracy is the rotation of power. Perfect!

In an article written in the Colorado Springs Gazette (Colorado) newspaper on October 30, 2008, the writer H. Blaine Miller wrote "…(the elected President) will become our Commander in Chief regardless of perceived qualifications or shortcomings. He will become America's new face to the world, regardless of whether we chose to vote for him or not. As such, he will deserve our respect not because he won an election but because he is our President. Many have taken to demonizing our current President for numerous personal shortcomings and certainly questionable political decisions….. While anyone is entitled to disagree with Presidential action, few maintain a respect for the office of the President once held by most in this country, the person who holds this office is the leader of the free world and his or her rank must be appreciated—for the sake of decency, reverence to our country and its Constitution, and simple American dignity. If we cannot find it within ourselves to respect our nation's highest office— regardless of its holder's personal shortcomings—then how are we to expect our global community to respect our country?….respect in spite of difference of opinion is truly a matter of maintaining the character of person and country…..regardless of who our new President-elect is to be, we should salute the rank and not the man. Our country's Constitution, character and future deserve no less." (2)

As an example of the negative thinking about America, there was a woman in Spanish class at a local language school, with whom Al and Biljana had struck a conversation. It was learned that she had emigrated from Scotland to the United States and was living in Ohio. She had come from a working family environment in her native country in which things were simple and constant. She moved to the United States and had been a naturalized citizen of America for twenty-two years by this time. She told Al and Biljana how she had come to America with very little and how she pulled herself up by her bootstraps to become successful. She was aggressive in the business she developed for herself within two years of arriving in Ohio. She saw an opportunity in real estate ownership. She took a chance, borrowed money from a bank on her very simple credit at the time, and purchased a house that she fixed up and sold for a profit. The notion caught on with her. As time progressed, she continued with the idea, and it eventually became successful. So successful, in fact, that she was able to create a company in which she did not have to work on a regular fulltime basis, and all went well.

During informal talks with the woman during school hours, Al and Biljana listened to her espouse her thinking about her situation in general. And, lo and behold, she kept putting down America! She complained about the taxes, about the health care system, about employees, about her government's imposed working conditions, all in a manner that sounded disparaging. She even kept referring to herself as being Scottish, not American, yet she held an American passport. She would talk about how great it was in Scotland. She was not able to give credit to the fact that she accomplished what she did because of her move to America. She couldn't see what had truly happened. She was actually denying her relationship with the facts!

Biljana says, "The woman just does not get it!" She was not in touch with the reality that a local American bank gave her credit without having much experience or collateral. She did not get the fact that the American system and circumstances allowed her to take these risks and attempt to better herself. She did not realize that her capabilities were being encouraged. She did not compare the situation with the one from which she emigrated—she appeared to ignore it.

Would she, in her former country, as a single woman, be assessed a good risk? Would she have been accepted as an aggressive business person? Would she have been able to climb up a business ladder to become successful and to offer employment to others? "Good questions" Biljana says after class one day, "and I think that she would not have emigrated to the United States if she had that same opportunity in Scotland."

Al and Biljana agree that there is no problem with the concept of criticizing our government and its officials or of using our freedom of speech, as those are foundations of our Country. Freedom of speech is probably the most cherished freedom in America, and Americans also know that in exercising that freedom, respect accorded to one's opinion is expected without that opinion being the one and only truth to the whole world. "But," Al says, "I do have a problem when there is a total denial of the facts and truth. It is like denying your mother, who gave birth to you and the opportunity to even exist."

In 1775, New York Supreme Court Judge Thomas Jones, who had been the attorney for the corporation of New York City stated "….Every man of industry and integrity has it in his power to live well, and many are the instances of persons who came here (to America) distressed by their poverty who now enjoy easy and plentiful fortunes."

Another example concerns an American man Al and Biljana met who had been living in New Zealand for many years working for a large company doing some sort of field work. He had now come to visit this part of Mexico to study Spanish for three months. In talking with him after class one day at the same language school, he made comments about the United States that were negative. He praised New Zealand and what it had to offer him. He was very pleased to be living there and had no intention of returning to the United States to live.

Al asked if he was an American or a New Zealander. His response was that he considered himself a New Zealander. Al and Biljana push him by asking "What passport do you have and use?" as this would define his true citizenship. His answer was as expected—"American."

The other obvious questions to ask him include: What was so great or different about living in New Zealand as compared to the U.S.? What would make you decide to live in another country? These specific questions were not asked of him, so there are no answers, only observations.

The next question directed at this man was the most important one, as far as Al and Biljana were concerned. "Would you become a citizen of New Zealand and give up your American citizenship?"

Well, the answer he gave to that question was what they expected—"No." The follow up question was also very important. "Why not?" His answer was astounding! "Why would I give up my American citizenship?"

Adlai Stevenson, American statesman, politician and two time candidate for President of the United States, said "understand that patriotism could rightly be defined as the celebration of 'the right to hold ideas that are different—the freedom of man to think as he pleases'." To this, Al adds, "This is acceptable and understood, but not to the detriment of America and its ideals."

Further, there was a young American couple they met that was taking an accelerated Spanish course at the same language school. Talking with them, Biljana learned the reason they were doing this was because their jobs in America required them to speak Spanish. So, here are Americans working in America, being paid by Americans, not being able to hold on to their jobs unless they can speak Spanish! What?

They worked for a social services agency of the U.S. Government in California, and the majority of the people they counseled did not speak English. Biljana also overheard the couple criticizing America by making statements to the effect that Americans were taking advantage of the Mexican workers because they were not willing to take some of the jobs the Mexicans were willing to take. And, even with this, the couple said that the U.S. Government was not giving these workers an opportunity to learn English, or forcing the employers to pay the workers a proper wage, or giving the workers some benefits. Here was Biljana, listening to these Americans speaking negatively about their own country, yet, not saying anything about the fact that the people they were supposed to be helping were not required to learn English or to follow the rules. What? Again, not right!

So, there Al and Biljana were, once again, with a situation that they not only did not understand, but could not discern any logical reasoning for the attitude. "If, in fact," Al says, "these other countries are so wonderful, so fulfilling, so satisfying, why hang on to the original citizenship? What are the reasons that a complete break cannot be made? What is so compelling about retaining something one won't need, doesn't respect, nor will use?"

4
PERSONAL EXPERIENCES

The time spent in Mexico was a wonderful part of the lives of Al and Biljana. They enjoyed the location, the people they met, the surroundings, the culture, the food, the language, the customs, the traditions. They would never change the fact they decided to make the move and that they would enjoy it as much as possible.

In their involvement and enjoyment with being residents of this city of some intrigue, Al and Biljana became aware of certain elements that they were learning about themselves. They felt they were more conscious and aware of their surroundings and how that affected their feelings.

For instance, they naturally developed a liking for certain local restaurants, not only for the food that was offered, but also the atmosphere. And, in their affection for these places, one element that was clear in their minds was that language was not a factor. There was no requirement in their thinking that anything had to be in English. They recognized that they were in a different situation than they were used to. The fact that some of the menus were in Spanish and the wait staff only spoke Spanish, and the prices were all in pesos, was more of a benefit than anything else, certainly more interesting. "After all," Biljana says, "this is Mexico and Mexican culture and we should respect that."

Popular restaurants they often visited were La Floresta, El Pirata, La Parilla, La Tarraya, Oscar and Lalo's. La Floresta was located on the main highway and serves the greatest fish tacos; El Pirata, which has the best and freshest ceviche ever tasted, is located way off the beaten path and was visited by local taxi drivers and politicians with no 'gringos' to be seen; La Parilla, is a very touristy place on the main strip and has wonderful tableside seafood grills; La Tarraya, directly on the beach and serves up fabulous Mexican fried whole fresh fish under palm trees; Oscar and Lalo's, which is about a half hour drive down a bumpy sand trail, is directly on the beach under palm trees and serves the most scrumptious variety of seafood imaginable on a large aluminum covered platter for several people to enjoy, including lobster, whole fried grouper, shrimp, pieces of fried barracuda, octopus, conch, ceviche, squid, rice, beans. Yum!

Since Al and Biljana enjoy fish and seafood, much of their diet consisted of it. The seafood sections of the larger markets were amazing in their size and content. However, it was sometimes impossible to ensure that the products were as fresh as one would think at this location.

After a relatively short period of time, their friends introduced them to Jose, a local fisherman. Jose spoke some English and was very friendly and very helpful, and even was willing to teach them some Spanish. He had a fish market popular with locals—bare painted walls, ceramic tile open cutting counters, water faucet, bare concrete floor, open to the world, plastic bags and they all worked in their swim trunks and bare feet. Upon befriending him, Al and Biljana could always get the freshest of fish—to the point where Jose would call them on the telephone when he had either grouper or snapper available. He would call on the telephone and simply say "I got snapper!" with no salutation nor explanation. Biljana would tell him how she wanted it cut up and drive over to pick it up. Great!

Jose would go out on an outboard motor driven large wooden dinghy with his spear gun, leaving about six in the morning. He would bring back the fresh fish about eleven, clean them, cut them the way requested and sell them at a very reasonable price. Why, when one time Al and Biljana visited the store, there was an eight foot bull shark lying on the floor waiting to be cut up! Wow! What a joy to deal with him!

As Al and Biljana became more acquainted with their new lifestyle and got more used to the ordinary and daily routine of living their lives, the attention and effort that was necessary for some of those seemingly simple everyday tasks of ordinary life became bothersome. And then, making comparisons with America seemed to become the norm for them.

Water, for instance. They knew that the water that came out of the taps was not for drinking. That had become obvious over the years they had visited Mexico prior to moving. They had even learned to ask, in restaurants and bars, if the water was pure—agua pura. But, the hassles they would go through to obtain potable water on a daily basis just for living purposes began to be a necessary nuisance.

They had to purchase, as everybody else did, distilled or artesian well water in various size closed containers. The five gallon size was delivered to their residence once or twice per week. The driver would ring the door bell to shout a query if any was needed, and an answer would be shouted back.

The men would carry up two to four bottles up three flights of stairs and place them in the kitchen. Al would then put the bottles in the closet, after checking to see if one of them had to be lifted and placed on top of the water dispenser. Sometimes there was an unseen crack on the bottle and there were incidences of some minor flooding on the kitchen floor.

The other types of bottled water purchased at the local markets came in two gallon and twenty ounce bottles, which were stored under the sink. The two gallon bottles were used to pour into a pitcher which was kept in the refrigerator. Some smaller bottles were kept in the refrigerator to be used when leaving the residence. The number of plastic bottles used by everybody was appalling; they all ended up in the trash or simply thrown on the streets and sidewalks, and even into the surrounding jungle.

It was also necessary to be involved with the local system of paying utility bills. In America, you receive the bill in the mail, write a check and send it back through the mails, or pay it online. Not in Mexico, or at least in this part of Mexico.

What had to be done was this: Al would go to the bank to take out cash, usually through the ATM machine, as only pesos were accepted; then Biljana would go to the Water Department building, the Electrical Department building and the Gas Company building to stand in line to pay the bills. The building locations were in all different parts of the city. Further, the bills came at different times of the month. Even further, the electric bill was delivered every two months, while all others were delivered every month. Sometimes, the bills weren't even delivered, which would lead to service being cut off. Now, try to get the service re-connected!

Purchasing the fabulous fruits and vegetables also created some additional work. Because the tap water was not potable, fruits and vegetables could not be safely washed with it. Therefore, disinfecting was a necessity. And, it did not matter if the fruits and vegetables were purchased from a local vendor, from the farmer, or from WalMart or Sam's Club. Fortunately, there were several disinfecting products available that could be utilized. It was a simple process, but, nonetheless, it was another necessary intrusion on time and effort.

Mail was another obstacle. The postal system in Mexico is not up to the standards that Al and Biljana were used to in America. In fact, it was practically non-existent. They never used it. Sometimes, local mail would arrive at their residence, but, only hand delivered by the maintenance man of the condominium complex. How it got into his hands was always a mystery. He would simply slip it under the door. If Al and Biljana had any mail to deliver to America, they would give it to somebody flying back to put in the mailbox at any airport. Conversely, any mail to be delivered to them had to be brought down by someone who came to visit. FedEx and UPS were an alternative, but not exactly dependable.

Besides the everyday annoyances, Al and Biljana had learned about other aspects of life living in this different culture. Some of these states of affairs were very disconcerting to them. It was disturbing to even hear about them, let alone be involved with them.

"Remember" Biljana says, "that we were told on several occasions about how to act in the unlikely event of a bad automobile accident?" The story is that, should anyone hit a person with an automobile, the best action to take is to continue driving! What?

The reasoning given to them was that the driver is financially liable to the injured for an indeterminate length of time. So, by leaving the accident, there is no liability, therefore, the driver's family is not beset with an unknown expense for an undetermined length of time. Unbelievable! The questions are, "Could you really do that? Could you leave the scene? Could you ignore the injured person?"

Fortunately, Al and Biljana never had to deal with this. To their knowledge, neither did any of their friends and acquaintances.

The condominium project that Al and Biljana lived in was basically no different than any other complex. It had common areas, landscaping, pool, parking areas, a maintenance man, rules and regulations, a homeowner's association and monthly dues. It had, also, a property manager and a board of directors, known locally as a Vigilante Committee, ostensibly to oversee all expenses and the property manager.

Well, it was not uncommon in this setting to have a property manager managing the money more for their personal benefit than the complex's needs. In Mexico, there is no overall regulated professional organization that has laws, rules of ethics and liability concerns that govern the property manager industry. This, obviously, opens the door to impropriety.

This happened to be the case for Al and Biljana. The property manager was operating the property as he saw fit, not based on any regulations or logic. For instance, even after agreeing to a specific contract for work to be done, additional money out of the bank account was spent by the manager such that it seemed that kickbacks to the property manager by the contractor were in order.

A case in point that directly happened to Al and Biljana can illustrate this phenomenon. Biljana says to Al while scrutinizing the monthly bills, "Do you remember when we had our electricity cut off when we came to visit our condominium before we moved?" Al remembered vividly because there seemed to be no excuse for such an episode.

They had been in the habit of paying the condominium dues in advance, sometimes by as much as six months, during a visit. They had also attempted to pay their monthly dues on time by long distance before moving to Mexico. And, because they would be away from Mexico for some time prior to moving, they talked to the property manager and were given a bank account number to which to wire the money so that everything would be timely. This is where things went so wrong.

It turned out that the account number was not correct, and the property manager would not update the information for them. This went on for several months, after which it was agreed upon that Al and Biljana would send money by Western Union. They did so, but the property manager would not bother to pick up the money. The idea was, as Al and Biljana saw it, that by not picking up the money to put into the account, that late fees would be attached. And, because of the late fees not being paid, the account would be delinquent, and further, that the property manager could then extract more money. With the monthly dues at $50 each month, and with the late fees for that six month period, it all added up to $1,500 according to the manager's accounting. There was no rhyme nor reason for such a number because the numbers just did not add up.

So, in their attempt to find out why there was no electricity in the condominium, they learned that the property manager had turned off the power at the electric meter, which is behind locked doors, ostensibly for non-payment. Further, Al and Biljana learned that it is illegal for anyone to turn off the power other than the electric company (government) itself. Since there was no delinquency on the electric account, the power did not need to be cut off. And, since Al and Biljana had prepaid the electric account at the company, eventually the power was restored—all through the actions of Al and Biljana, certainly not the property manager's efforts, after many days with no air conditioning or refrigeration!

Yet another incident that was disturbing to hear concerned lawyers, judges and the courts. It so happened that a local businessman with whom they were acquainted had fired one of his employees for stealing, selling drugs from the store and not being on the job at all times for which he was hired. After a few months, the employee sued the businessman for being fired. "Haven't we been told of this scenario before?" Al says. In spite of the fact that the businessman had been generous to the employee by giving bonuses, signing documents verifying the employee's employment so he could get a bank loan and allowing him to have flexible work hours, the frivolous lawsuit was filed.

During the several months of meetings, court appearances, delays and attempts at compromise, the businessman's patience had come to an end. So, at yet another court appearance, the businessman approached the former employee's lawyer in the hall of the courthouse. He explained to the lawyer that his client had no money and that he probably will lose the case. Therefore, the lawyer will not get any money for his efforts. So, the businessman asked the lawyer what it would take to have the case thrown out at this court appearance. They agreed on a price, and the lawyer went into the courtroom, talked to the judge and the case was dismissed! Can this really happen? Is this the way things are in such places? This showed to Al and Biljana, just how vulnerable foreigners were to the whims of the culture.

As more time progressed, Al and Biljana noticed that almost every time some sort of date or schedule was made with the locals, the set time was ignored. Now, they both knew that being sociably late is acceptable. They were prepared for such happenings, but not to the level that was prevalent in their new found home. It is acceptable to be, maybe, one half hour late to some social event. Understandable. But, because of the frequency and depth of such behavior now being realized, the frustration level crept in at the beginning of their stay in Mexico.

However, they learned that the local acceptable limit was way beyond anything that even made sense. There were many instances for them, where the schedule, or date, would be one hour, two hours, three hours, difference. And, there would be no contact to give any explanation. In fact, upon showing up at the late time, there was no apology or explanation. This was true of politicians, professionals, tradespeople, workers, sales people.

The problem for Al and Biljana was that they were used to being on time. So, whenever some schedule was agreed upon, they would show up within the respectable one half hour grace period, only to find that the hosts or the event wasn't even ready to begin! And, then embarrassment would appear on both sides. This posture actually was so prevalent, that even some scheduled public events, such as performances by music groups or politicians or sports, were not immune to such lateness.

To further illustrate this point, Al reminded Biljana of the incident concerning some friends of theirs. The American couple had purchased a piece of property in Playa del Carmen upon which they wished to construct a house. During a visit to the site, they agreed on the price, the terms, the schedule, and paid a deposit to purchase the property. Their local attorney told them that the final paperwork would take several weeks to prepare. Fine.

After being home for a couple of weeks, they telephoned their attorney and asked about the progress of the papers. They were told that the papers would be ready in two weeks. They agreed that on a Thursday at 11am they would meet in the attorney's office to sign all the documents and make the final payment.

The couple made airplane reservations, hotel accommodations

and all arrangements to be there at the scheduled time, and everything was set. "Remember," Al says, "they had to reset their business schedules, client relationships, personal demands and obligations to accommodate the timetable."

They dutifully showed up at the attorney's office at 11am on that Thursday, only to be told by the secretary that the attorney was not in just yet. So, being patient people, they sat and waited. After two hours, they asked the secretary to phone the attorney and ask what was happening, and were told that the attorney was on her way to the office and would be there at 4pm.

After 4pm, they were told that the attorney was not going to be in the office that day. So, they agreed that they would meet the next day at 2pm.

The next day, predictably, they showed up at 2PM, and the attorney was not there. The secretary told them the attorney would be about an hour late. Finally, the attorney arrived, ushered the couple into an office, and completed the transaction.

Now, the end of this story is that, not only did the attorney not arrive on the original scheduled meeting day, and that she did not arrive at the rescheduled time and day, she offered no apology, nor any explanation. She simple went on with the business as if nothing happened. Obviously, the couple was furious about the whole situation, and they never hired her again. After all, they said, it was the attorney who set the date, day and time for the original meeting.

Al and Biljana, through this incident, then came up with a true definition of the Mexican term "manana." They had heard through the years, and had learned in their study of Spanish, that "manana" means tomorrow. Not true! The real meaning of the word to Al and Biljana, is "not now? It does not go any farther than that. It only means that something will happen after this moment, at an unspecified time. Wow!

Then, Biljana reminds Al of an additional annoyance. The scenario a person goes through just to put gasoline in a car—as happened to them a few times. In Mexico, all of the gas stations are owned by a government monopoly called Pemex. Therefore, whenever one wants gasoline, there is only one brand to buy, and there are many stations available. Not much is computerized and credit cards are not accepted or used, so an attendant helps with the process because one does not fill one's own tank, and he/she expects a tip, which is generally offered. "So" Al says, "you tell the attendant how many pesos worth of which octane you want, and he/she goes to work." And, when one is not Mexican, or has foreign or rental car license plates, "the game begins."

The attendant begins talking to the buyer, in Spanish, maybe a little English, and generally asks how much was paid for the car. Then he/she begins to roll the eyes, make a gesture of much money, and shows a level of envy.

After the peso amount for the gasoline is reached, the buyer hands the attendant the pesos, which is either exactly correct, or with change coming. During this exchange, sometimes the attendant adds a little magic. By talking and gesturing and asking questions, the buyer is slightly distracted, and the attendant somehow, magically, switches the amount of pesos to something smaller—like a 20 peso note instead of the 200 peso note given to him. So, satisfied with the payment, the buyer begins to walk away.

"Now" Al says, "the attendant/magician stops and says that you didn't give him the correct peso note, and shows the lower value note. As a foreigner, you are bewildered, try to figure it out and absentmindedly give him another note. This game is well thought out, well practiced and well carried out. It is yet another method of extracting money from strangers."

37

Another nifty method of extorting money by these same attendants concerns the gas cap. Since it is the attendant that does all of the work to put gas in the tank, he has control of the gas cap. So, he can simply close the door after putting gas in, let you pay, and let you take off driving without your gas cap. After smelling gasoline and checking the situation, you return to the station to get the "forgotten" gas cap. The attendant then cannot find yours, so he offers another one. Only, to receive the cap, you have to pay him money! After all, it is not your original cap, but somebody else's.

The key here is that even such a simple task as refueling an automobile one must be alert and aware. In this case, getting out of the car and standing by while the gas is being poured, and then being certain about payment, becomes a necessity. What a bother!

Al and Biljana wanted to have internet service for their computer in their condominium. They had learned that the best company to use for it was the local cable television company called Cablemas. Cablemas could provide cable for television, internet service and telephone land line.

Al visited the main office to ask for the service. He was told by the lady at the service desk that the cables and wires are not in his area of the City, therefore, the service was unavailable. Now, Al knew better, because his friend in the same complex, on the same street, had the service.

But, he left the office frustrated, because he knew he would get nowhere with the people there (through his experience of having lived there for one and one half years already).

A short time thereafter, he looked out his condo window and saw two Cablemas trucks on his street. He went downstairs to talk with the supervisor of the trucks, found he spoke some English, and asked him if he could get the service to the condominium. The supervisor said he can do it. Al told the man he will pay him some money if he can do it while he is there. He paid the money, the men got to work, and, Voila! Al had internet service.

Besides the obvious questions and possible answers, the most amazing part about this showed up as yet another mystery—every month after the installation, Al got his Cablemas bill delivered to his door! No problem with paying for it, just an unidentifiable situation to explain and to determine how the main office knew of the installation. After all, didn't the main office say the service was not available?

By living in Mexico, as Al and Biljana are sure is true in other countries, one becomes aware of the exchange rate. This was a new phenomenon for them.

There are many places to exchange dollars to pesos—banks, shops, small exchange outlets (cambios). It is easy to do, and the tiny cambios are located everywhere.

However, determining that value of the exchange is bothersome. The rates change, it seems, hourly. So, depending on where you wish to do the transaction, along with the time of the day, the amounts vary. Sometimes, you make a good deal, and sometimes it's not so good. Keeping up with the value of your money becomes sort of a game, and a topic of discussion among friends.

Also, a very curious aspect of this exchanging process comes into play. When exchanging money to pesos in a bank, the teller requires you to show your passport. Now, "What does the passport have to do with cash?" Biljana asks, "What is the relationship?" This is very weird because in no other situation, do you have to show a passport—like the shops and the cambios. Besides, what local resident carries around his passport for no reason? Very annoying.

Another part of this same situation that is peculiar is that the prices for items and services don't change along with the variation in money exchange. This means that sometimes a purchase has more worth than other times. Talk about confusing!

During their stay in Mexico it became obvious to Al and Biljana that how Americans live has become the norm and necessary for the local inhabitants. Shortly before Al and Biljana moved into their condominium, a Sam's Club was constructed and opened not too far from them. This became not only an instant success, but a basis for what the locals would demand from businesses and other ventures, in terms of value, presentation, selection and comfort.

So, as time progressed while living in the condominium, they saw a tremendous growth in American style offerings. A WalMart was constructed right in the middle of the city and was instantly a success. What they saw being added to the local marketplace was McDonald's, Burger King, Subway, Starbucks, Domino's Pizza, Papa John's Pizza, Hagen Daaz Ice Cream, Dairy Queen, Woolworth's, ReMax Real Estate, Coldwell-Banker Real Estate and Stewart Title Company. All of this was helpful to the ex-patriots living in Mexico and have since become a part of life for all others.

There had been only one movie theater in town when they moved there. It was a typical old time facility on the second floor of a relatively new commercial building in the middle of the city with very little parking for cars. Now, there were two new fully air-conditioned shopping malls constructed on the periphery of the downtown area that featured new theaters. They were typically American—multi-theater configurations, stadium seating, adjustable seats, surround sound, adequate and clean restrooms, popcorn and parking. The movies were mostly American, in English with Spanish sub-titles.

It was obvious to Al and Biljana that as all of this was happening the quality of services and respect for consumers was raising the bar for all of the inhabitants of the area. Al notes, "This bringing of competition and employment is in turn helping the locals and visitors alike."

The local supermarkets then updated their facilities to be able to continue as competition. Everybody was happy.

Through their own experience, Al and Biljana became aware of what seemed to be a contradiction in how the public was protected as consumers. They noticed that the state and federal licensing laws for many professions were somewhat erratic or not in force at all. Hair stylists, engineers and taxi drivers had to be licensed, sometimes after apprenticeship. Real estate brokers and agents, architects and property managers did not have to be licensed. How is the public protected from illegal and improper transactions?

What this did to Al and Biljana and to others, is that they then could not believe anyone. Trust disappeared. Everyone immediately is thought of in terms of "what can go wrong, or, what is it that they want, or, what will they do to me." So, the people who live in this context, who are not part of the basic culture, always have their defenses up and ask questions of themselves, "How do I protect myself? Is no one's word good?"

This brought up another memory to Al. Some years ago, he went on a scuba diving trip to the Bay Islands of Honduras. During his time there, he took the opportunity to visit the small town on the island of Roatan. As he wandered around the streets and shops, he became aware of something he had never seen before. "I noticed," he relates to Biljana "that there were soldiers in uniform walking around with rifles. This was something I had never before experienced." He went on to explain that it was a little unnerving and it stuck in his mind. And, now, he was seeing the same thing in Mexico, which continued to be bothersome.

Biljana then reminded Al of another circumstance that happened to the both of them several years earlier. She asks "Do you remember our trip to Sarajevo in Bosnia? That was also a memorable experience for us, wasn't it?"

In recalling the visit, Al remembered some of the feelings and observations during that two week stay that were parallel to their thinking at this time. It was uncanny how, revealed only after their Mexico experience that events, expectations and methods were comparable. So, they began talking about what they remembered. They learned that the Bosnians at one time had asked for help from America—to prevent the killing of their people by the Serbs. They were asking America and NATO, for money, for protection, safety, etc.

Al and Biljana's scenario started at the airport upon arrival in Sarajevo. They felt uneasy as they were ushered into the secure immigration area. It seemed so unfriendly and sparse. After going through the entry process, which was actually not so bad because Biljana spoke the language, they were flagged down by an unknown man who quietly moved them into a car waiting outside. The man had identified himself as a representative of the mayor of a local suburb, which is exactly as Biljana's brother told them he would arrange.

Now, Al and Biljana had expected some sort of official recognition due to the reasons for them being in Sarajevo. Biljana's brother had made all of the arrangements which included meetings with the mayor of the suburb because there was a supposed need for an American engineer/architect to help with a multi-national train project to be constructed in the mayor's suburb. So, a certain amount of upper level greeting and ceremony was thought to be in order.

During their visit, Al and Biljana saw some things that disturbed them, but were not completely aware of at the time. Some events seemed strange, certainly out of the norm for them.

There were, for instance, areas of the city that were officially off limits to all people. There were fenced off sections with signs on them in several languages, warning that there were land mines still in the ground. There were military trucks, mostly with SFOR written on them (which was the international military force), driving all around the city with armed soldiers in them. There were buildings that had obviously been bombed and shelled that were still in very bad shape, even with some areas of them with people living in them. There were occupied areas of the city that were off limits to certain citizens, which were designated by signs.

There was a specific incident where Al and Biljana went to visit a former Bosnian army general friend of Biljana's brother. The visit was in the General's apartment, which was close to where there had been fighting between the Bosnian army and the Serbian army during the war. The visit was very nice and cordial, but there seemed to be an underlying uneasy feeling in the apartment. Al concluded that it had to do with the idea that the General, with his wife, were living so close to the area where he had been fighting a war just a short time earlier—where there was violence and death and destruction. There seemed also to be an insecure feeling, not one of peace and tranquility.

What Al and Biljana gleaned out of all of these incidents and stories, is that a person cannot fully trust any information that is given to him by anyone, in Mexico at least. "What makes it even worse," Al says to Biljana, "is that no one is immune to this type of behavior. It is possible that everyone is capable of acting this way, or giving this type of information, or turning on you for no logical reason."

With their move to Mexico, and their visit to Sarajevo, along with the experience in Honduras, they became aware of how this singular observation was something that was very different from what they have and enjoy in America. Safety and security, maybe?

5
PRIDE

Al and Biljana had a difficult time with all of this. As Americans, they were proud of their backgrounds. It was easy and pleasant for Al to say that he is American with Russian born parents. Biljana would say with delight that she is an American with Yugoslavian background. Pride showed through in both arenas. They believed that being proud of their heritage was very important. However, as for their nationality, they were Americans, first and foremost. They believed that their parents would not only agree with this, but, they would shine in their thoughts about it.

The pride that Al and Biljana had for recognizing their convictions and beliefs about America and being patriotic went beyond just for themselves. They instilled their ideas into their three children. As the children grew, they were taught that hard work with high moral and ethical standards, along with education, will be rewards that will pay in the short and long runs.

As the children grew into adulthood, they had no fear of working hard to gain what they needed and wanted. They all asked for, and received, higher education because they knew that it was important, and a privilege to possess to go on to higher things in life. They were taught to recognize that these efforts were available to them because they were brought up in America, where these opportunities abound. To take advantage of these potentials was a fact of life which should not be dismissed.

And, they were taught that the right of Americans to protest in a legal manner was acceptable, that to vote was a necessity, that to follow the laws of the land was proper and necessary, and that to voice their opinions was more than acceptable. By taking this pattern of thinking and living in America, lessons were learned and practiced.

Biljana says, "We all, as parents, wish and expect that our children will live a better, safer and easier life than we do." Natural assumption. We, as parents, work toward that ideal. We sacrifice, work hard, and give attention to our children, directing them so that life is good. We want them to have things we didn't or couldn't have. We wish it and work for it.

With this in mind, there were other instances of negative thinking when Al and Biljana talked to some younger Americans who were visiting Mexico for various reasons—education, experience, to sow wild oats. It was surprising to hear what they were saying about America and being American. Shocking, in fact! It seemed that some of the critics of America in foreign countries were Americans! How dare they infer that America is actually trying to take over other countries to make them into other 'Americas'?

An arrival by America into other countries would be about a concern for human rights issues for all peoples and/or criminal activities, such as 9/11, that interfere with America.

We Americans understand and enjoy the concept of true freedom of speech. But, when this concept is taken out of our Country, it may not be accepted in the same manner, mood or extent. An American's personal statement in other locations may not be taken as a personal opinion only; it may be taken as a universal American truth. We Americans understand the idea that my truth may not be your truth. Do other peoples?

Al and Biljana believe that America allows people to do things for their families as they wish so long as it is civilized and within the law. One thing they learned about this idea, however, is that it seems possible to give too much. Some of the younger Americans they talked to in Mexico seemed to expect to be given too much. They were taking so much for granted, possibly, because it was given to them by their parents. So, it seems that giving so much is a two edged sword. Does this give these young people permission to criticize their own country? Wow! What a revelation! How hurtful! It is their right, but is it correct?

One of Al's very best friends in Colorado was Apollo 15 Astronaut Colonel James B. Irwin, the eighth man to walk on the moon. After Jim's return from the moon, he set up a non-denominational Christian organization he called High Flight Foundation. Through this Foundation, Jim was able to travel all over the world by invitation to spread the word of the Foundation. He visited heads of states, kings, queens, emperors, even dictators. Upon his return to Colorado Springs after each trip, Jim would get in touch with Al to talk about various subjects; space travel, skiing, hiking, family. Jim commented on many occasions with this remark—"No matter where I go, or who I visit, it is always best to come home. There is no place like America."

The Governor of California, Arnold Schwartzenegger, has stated "I began dreaming of coming to America when I was ten years old, because it has no rival as the land of opportunity."

Then, there is an anecdote that Al and Biljana heard about this very subject. It seems that a self important college freshman walking along the beach took it upon himself to explain to a senior citizen resting on some steps why it was impossible for the older generation to understand his generation. "You grew up in a different world, actually, almost a primitive one" the student said loud enough for others to hear. "The young people of today grew up with television, jet planes, space travel, men walking on the moon. We have nuclear energy, ships and cell phones, computers with lightning speed.... and much more." After a brief silence, the senior citizen responded as follows. "You're right son. We didn't have those things when we were young....so, we invented them. Now, you arrogant little s__t, what are you doing for the next generation?"

With all of this, these younger people were talking about how bad our government handles the business of government—the economy, the wars in the Middle East, the politicians, lack of affordable healthcare, the political and economic situation in other countries and the effect on us and the environment.

Oh, especially the environment! What Al and Biljana became acutely aware of in Mexico was the lack of pride, or possibly lack of education in the physical surroundings of the local area. There was trash everywhere—plastic bottles, diapers, paper, animal excrement, garbage—and very few people seemed to be bothered by it. When Al and Biljana drove across the border back into America, they became instantly aware of the difference in just this singular state of affairs. Wow!

This bothered Al and Biljana to no end. They constantly were trying to understand it. They felt that there must be some method of getting all people to have a better understanding and acceptance of the uniqueness that America is and has been since its inception, and, how America takes the high road to impart this knowledge to other parts of the world.

6
WHAT AMERICA IS

Al and Biljana became aware that most people in the world do not know, and/or ignore, the fact that America donates more people, money, expertise, ideas and supplies (as a government and as individual citizens) to other countries than any other nation in the world, not to mention the American lives that have been lost in those endeavors.

America is the only country that has defeated enemies at war, and then went into those same defeated countries and re-built them for the use of their own citizens—with American people, money, supplies, effort and sacrifices—even to the point that those countries became business competition to America. And, since the Spanish-American War in 1898, the wars were without an attempt to enlarge the area and control of the United States. Wars were entered into by America to help rid the world of despotism, to safeguard life, to try to end man's inhumanity to man. Not for expansion. Not for colonization. In fact, after both World War I and World War II, America's allies held onto lands that were conquered in Europe, while America took none.

See the following timeline:

TIMELINE OF U.S. WARS AND CONFLICTS

1775-1783—Revolutionary War between English Colonists and Great Britain:
For independence to create the United States of America.

1798-1800—Franco-American Naval War between the United States and France:
To end the seizing of American ships trading with Britain and France's refusal to receive the United States Minister.

1801-1805; 1815—Barbary Wars between the United States and Morocco, Algiers, Tunis, Tripoli:
To defend American interests in the region after Tripoli declared war on the United States.

1812-1815- War of 1812 between the United States and Great Britain:
To end the British impressment of American sailors into the Royal Navy and the interception of neutral ships and blockades of the United States during British hostilities with France.

1836—War of Texas Independence between Texas and Mexico:
Texians became disillusioned with the Mexican government and wanted changes in immigration, judicial and political policies as they were used to the rights of the United States such as Freedom of Religion.

1846-1848—Mexican War between the United States and Mexico:
Due to failure of resolving the boundary dispute, aid was given for the voluntary annexation of Texas to the United States. With the Treaty of Guadelupe Hidalgo in 1848, parts of Colorado, Kansas, Oklahoma, New Mexico, Wyoming, California, Nevada, Utah

were ceded to the United States and the border between Mexico and the United States was established at the Rio Grande River. Mexico was paid $18,250,000.

1861-1865—Civil War between the Union and the Confederacy:

To settle differences between ideologies of Americans.

1898—Spanish—American War between the United States and Spain:

After Spain relinquished its sovereignty, aid in the wars of independence for Cuba, the Philippines and Puerto Rico, and annexed under the Treaty of Paris in 1898.

1914-1918—World War I between the United States, Britain, France and Germany, Italy, Austria-Hungary:

After Germany's submarine warfare against neutral shipping and to rid the world of political transgression.

1939-1945—World War II between the United States, Great Britain, France, Russia and Germany, Italy, Japan.

To rid the world of political transgression and the degradation of human rights.

1950—1953—Korean War between South Korea, the United States and North Korea, Communist China:

To prevent the spread of Communism.

1960-1975—Vietnam War between South Vietnam, The United States and North Vietnam:

To prevent the spread of Communism.

1961—Bay of Pigs Invasion between the United States and Cuba:

To prevent the threat of a Communist takeover of a territory so close to the United States.

1963—Grenada—intervention by the United States:

To prevent the increased threat of Soviet and Cuban influence in the region after the development of an international airport on the island by Russia.

1969—Invasion of Panama between the United States and Panama:

To protect United States' historical rights to the Panama Canal from Noriega's attempt to take it.

1990-1991—Persian Gulf War between the United States, Coalition Forces and Iraq:

To search for weapons of mass destruction as developed by Saddam Hussein.

1995-1996—Bosnia and Herzegovina between the United States, NATO forces and Serbia:

To prevent the takeover of Balkan countries by Serbia and their suppression of Muslims.

2001—Attack on the World Trade Center in New York:

To locate and punish the Taliban and Al-Qaeda perpetrators of this unprovoked incursion on the United States.

2001—Invasion of Afghanistan between the United States, Coalition Forces and the Taliban:

To contain the effects of the extremist Islamists in threats of worldwide violence and the United States.

2003—Invasion of Iraq between the United States, Coalition Forces and Iraq:

To contain the effects of the extremist Islamists in their effort to dominate the religious and political world.

Al then developed his thoughts about just how far America has gone to help and protect other nations of the world. The one thing that stood out to him was that so many Americans gave their lives so other nations could be free. What a revelation! Talk about getting a reality check!

He offers to Biljana the following query: "There are cemeteries in other countries where American military personnel are buried in tribute to their ultimate sacrifice in the name of peace and security. There are American military cemeteries in the

Netherlands, Luxembourg, France, Italy, England, Belgium, Mexico, Panama, the Philippines and in Tunisia. Do you suppose there are cemeteries in the United States commemorating the fallen of foreign military located in America?" Biljana replies, "No, I am sure there are none." And, there are in fact, none. This is a further testament which shows that America is strong and has the capability to prevent any ideas by others for takeover or conquest. With this in mind, it is a further characterization of what America stands for and what America has done for others. Is there a thank you?

Thomas Jefferson is quoted as saying, "If there is one principle deeply rooted in the mind of every American, it is that we should have nothing to do with conquest."

CHRONOLOGICAL LIST OF U.S. EXPANSION(3)
As adapted from an article by Franklin K. Van Zandt.

DATE	TERRITORY	NOTES
1783	Former 13 Colonies	Treaty of Paris of 1783 following American Revolutionary War
1803	Louisiana Purchase	Purchased from France for $15 million, including assumed claims
1819	Florida (East & West)	Purchased from Spain for $5 million in assumed claims under Adams-Onis Treaty
1845	Texas	Annexation of independent republic
1846	Oregon Territory	Oregon Treaty with Great Britain
1848	Mexican Cession	Purchased from Mexico following American-Mexican War: $15 million plus $3.25 million in assumed claims
1853	Gadsden Purchase	Purchased from Mexico for $10 million
1857	Baker Island Howland Island Navassa Island	Unincorporated territory claimed under Guano Act of 1856
1858	Jarvis Island Johnston Atoll	Unincorporated territory claimed under Guano Act of 1856
1867	Alaska	Purchased from Russia for $7.2 million
186?	Midway Islands	Unincorporated territory claimed under Guano Act of 1856
1898	Hawaiian Islands	Annexation of independent republic
1898	Palmyra Atoll	Acquired with Hawaii
1898	Philippine Islands	Purchased from Spain for $20 million following Spanish-American War
1898	Puerto Rico Guam	Annexed following Spanish-American War
1898	American Samoa	Annexed in settlement with Britain and Germany
1899	Wake Island	Annexation of unoccupied area
1903	Panama Canal Zone	Leased from Panama for $10 million, plus $250,000 annually
1917	U.S. Virgin Islands	Purchased from Denmark for $25 million
1922	Kingman Reef	Annexed
194?	Northern Mariana Islands	United Nations Trust Territory
1947	Federated States of Micronesia	United Nations Trust Territory
194?	Republic of Palau	United Nations Trust Territory
194?	Republic of the Marshall Islands	United Nations Trust Territory

The Thursday, February 19, 2009, edition of the Colorado Springs, Colorado, newspaper, The Gazette, had an article written by columnist Barry Fagin, Senior Fellow at The Independence Institute, entitled, "People want to believe in government," in which was stated in part, "The pride of other nations notwithstanding, America is a world leader, not just militarily but economically and politically. Newly formed nations form tripartite governments, like America. They send their best and brightest to American universities. They may not like everything we do, and they may put their own spin on American institutions, but, ultimately, much of American ideas, culture and policy are imitated by other countries, including post communist Russia." (4).

"By the way, it is interesting to note some statistics about Nobel Prize winners," Al says to Biljana, and he continues: *"With a total of almost 600 university affiliated Nobel Prize winners, 279 of the graduates of American universities are from other countries. For instance, Harvard University with 28, Stanford University with 17, Massachusetts Institute of Technology with 15, University of Chicago with 15, California Institute of Technology with 14, University of California at Berkeley with 14, Columbia University with 12 and Princeton University with 11. Further, 75 percent of the Fields Medal (Nobel Prize medal for mathematics), also from other countries, served as professors in American universities."* According to these statistics, no other country comes close to these numbers.

Obviously, as time marched on during their time in Mexico, Al and Biljana made many friends. Sometimes they would sit on the beach or sit around a wood box or on a friend's boat with a drink and have serious discussions with some of them. In particular, one man, originally from Israel and who also had lived in

Germany and America, owned a large tourist and art shop on the main street. He was very engaging in his conversations and thoughts which he easily imparted to them. His comments seemed to always include some references to the quality and value of America. He would say that America was always at the forefront of most things that a civilized, modern country should have and stand for. Specifically, he referred to the progress in such arenas as business, international relations, communications, the acceptance of ideas, the availability of products and services, and so on. His praise of America was heartwarming. He stated that not only would he like to move to America, but he felt that everybody would like to live in America! Nice to hear!

A Mexican woman who became a very dear friend to Al and Biljana told them about herself and family. She originally came from Mexico City and now had a tourist type business in town. She lived in her own house, which she helped to build, with her children and animals. Lounging on the beach one typically sunny and warm day, she talked about how she would love to live in America. She had visited America many times and spoke English very well, and thought America would be the place for her.

She told the story about her brother, who was a very famous movie actor in Mexico. In short order, he decided that America was the place to do what he wished, and Hollywood was the location to do it. He moved, got into the industry and did very well for himself. He was more successful than he was in Mexico. In fact, his wife and children still live in California.

"Now, why would he move to America if he was successful in Mexico?," Al asks. The answer was simple. "He could do more, be more creative, expand his abilities in the profession he chose," says his sister.

Then, Al and Biljana became aware of something else of great importance. Namely, that other countries are basically selfish and greedy. Those countries not only accepted, with glee, what America gave them; they demanded it, they became dependent upon what was given, without even a thank you or a kiss on the cheek or a wave of the hand.

Scholar Joseph Nye, PhD, University Distinguished Service Professor at the Kennedy School of Government at Harvard University is quoted as referring to a: "….widespread desire to emigrate to the United States, the prestige and corresponding high proportion of foreign students at U.S. universities, and the spread of U.S. styles of popular music and cinema….."

A further realization came to the fore—when there was some sort of natural disaster or national or international event that befell America, very few of the other countries offered help—in any form! Wow! Talk about selfish! Talk about not being able, not willing to volunteer, to give! Talk about being blind!

Is it true that the United States sends more than $21 billion dollars (that is $21 with nine zeros)—or $3,300 for each American—per year of its citizen's hard earned money out of the country to other peoples? For a typical family of four, that comes to $13,200 per year. When one considers that the poverty level is $21,065 per year, this is appalling.

The Washington File of the Bureau of International Information Programs of the United States Department of State reports that in fiscal year 2007, the total foreign aid cost was $21.3 billion dollars. (6)

PARTIAL LIST OF RECIPIENTS—U.S. DOLLAR

Iraq $522,000,000
Afghanistan $962,000,000
Jordan $468,000,000
West Bank/Gaza $80,000,000
Andean Counterdrug Initiative $704,000,000
Former Soviet Union Republics $371,000,000
Eastern Europe/Baltic States $228,000,000
Indonesia $75,000,000
Israel $2,500,000,000
Egypt $1,800,000,000
Sudan $450,000,000
Pakistan $942,000,000
Multi-Lateral Development Assistance $1,300,000,000
International Financial Institutions $1,300,000,000
Migration & Refugee Assistance $750,000,000
Trade Capacity Enhancement Fund $522,000,000
International Financial Institutions $1,300,000,000
Migration & Refugee Assistance $750,000,000
Trade Capacity Enhancement Fund $522,000,000

Al says to Biljana, "You know when we read that people criticize America for not sending its share of aid to others, it really bothers me. Let's look at the statistics in terms of dollars, not percentages. In the year 2007, the United Kingdom spent $12.4 billion, France—$10.6 billion, Germany—$10.4 billion, Japan—$7.5 billion, Netherlands—$5.5 billion, Sweden—$3.9 billion, Canada—$3.9 billion, Spain—$3.8 billion and Italy—$3.6 billion. This shows that even with a smaller percentage of America's budget, more actual money is given away by Americans than any other country."

What is additionally critical to understand, is that this money which comes out of the government's budget does not include all of the money and effort that goes around the world as personally donated by Americans. Since America volunteers and donates more of everything than any other country, this added benefit seems to be forgotten by the world. According to the 2006 Index of Global Philanthropy, private donations amounted to $71 billion. "And," Biljana continues, "that amount is not included in the government's expenditure. So, what does that all total?" Is there grand total somewhere?

"Now, possibly," Al continues, "where the money goes and what it is used for needs to be re-thought." At the World Economic Forum in New York in February, 2002, United States Senator Patrick Leahy noted that "two thirds of U.S. government aid goes to only two countries: Israel and Egypt. Much of the remaining third is used to promote U.S. exports or to fight a war against drugs that could only be won by tackling drug abuse in the U.S." Are our priorities right? Could we get more bang for the buck by making changes?

While lounging on the futon in the second bedroom of their condo, Al remembered The Truman Doctrine, which was pertinent to this thinking. President Harry S Truman, in 1947, established that the United States would provide political, military and economic assistance to all democratic nations under threat from external or internal authoritarian forces.

He requested that Congress provide $400,000,000 worth of aid to both the Greek and Turkish governments at that time. Truman argued that Communism in the Greek War would endanger the stability of Turkey which would undermine the political stability of the Middle East, where America had major interests. Also, the spread of authoritarianism would undermine the foundations of international peace and hence the security of the United States.

It subsequently became the policy of the United States to support free peoples who are resisting attempted subjugation by armed minorities or by outside pressures. This was a sharp break with the traditional avoidance by the United States of extensive foreign commitment beyond the Western Hemisphere during peacetime, because the Doctrine was deemed to be in the best interest of the United States.

Sometimes, even good intentioned Americans fail to appreciate their country. On one of their many trips to Cancun to do some additional shopping for items not available locally, about an hour away (that time when husband and wife have conversations that cannot be ignored because they are locked in a car for a period of time) Al says to Biljana, "You know, there was a story many years ago, about an American coastal city that was dependent primarily on the presence of the military as its major local industry. The Navy had been there for years as the main employer of the citizens. After some time, the citizens began to complain and moan about the sailors monopolizing the business district and the many amenities and services the city offered." He continues, "The complaining became a regular and annoying occurrence amongst the citizens. And, eventually, the citizens became hostile toward the sailors."

Biljana queries Al, "What happened?"

"The military came up with the idea of paying the sailors in two dollar bills, instead of the regular method. The city was inundated with the two dollar bills, and came to realize the importance of the sailors for the welfare of the city and its citizens." He says. "This changed the sentiments of the locals."

If it were possible, Al and Biljana discussed, to do something similar in the present day circumstance, would there be the same outcome? "Good question." they say to each other.

As they thought about this idea, and talked about it, a scenario began to evolve. Taking into account the factual history of America's willingness to volunteer and donate, adding it to the story of non-appreciation by the story of the American coastal city, reiterating the stories about the Scottish woman, the man living in New Zealand, the couple studying Spanish, and combining it all with the attitude of other countries—should the government of the United States take some drastic action to perk up the lazy attitude of other countries and peoples? Is America being subverted by those who do not think? What can the United States do to get the other countries to say "Thank you"?"

How can it be carried out such that other countries willingly give of themselves when the need in America arises? What can Americans do to regain their rightful place in the world as the world leader? After all, we damn well deserve it!

7
POSSIBILITIES

The next perplexing question was then forthcoming. Why is it that some young Americans are so eager to talk about America without giving credit to what America and Americans have done around the world? Is it possible that volunteering and donating can actually work against you? How is it that helping has become interfering?

Al's idea was, in his mind, simple. He says "Let us, the United States, tell the world that we need to strengthen and fix our own internal problems for the time being. If we, America, took time off for, say two years, from the volunteering and donating to other countries, and concentrated on ourselves during that time, what would happen? Then, after the two year period, go back to being the parents of the rest of the world."

"What would happen, in your mind?" Biljana asks.

As a preface to his answer, Al says, "When I listen to politicians talking politically and analysts talking analytically about how much money is spent by America on foreign aid, all I hear is the percentage of the overall United States budget that is used for this line item. They talk about it being less than 1%, or that it is 0.7%, or some such percentage. If we were all smart, we would think in terms of numbers of dollars instead of percentages. So, if 0.7% of the budget equals more than $12 billion dollars, it would make more of an impact on each of us. What this means to me is that we would realize how much good this amount of money would do for our own citizens. For instance, how much help would $12 billion dollars have been for the victims of hurricane Katrina in New Orleans? How much would be realized by spending $12 billion on our educational system? Or, our healthcare system? Or, our homeless situation?"

In order to answer, Al's thoughts would have to be in the form of political philosophy. And, there are some assumptions that have to be made. He says, "The method that scientists and deep thinkers use to study an hypothesis is by putting aside obvious and tried and true processes. Therefore, it is necessary for me to think outside of what would be considered normal. So, I will answer the question by looking at the situation head on with no thoughts of peripheral ideas, no mitigating circumstances, no outside influences, no political machinations. Simple—just thinking of us, America." Al realizes the value and benefit of international political and economic intercourse, but for this particular thinking, he overlooked these in order to be completely neutral.

"Some politicians and political pundits actually have an opposite approach." Al says. "They have already developed a result and then create the comments and arguments to prove the result." Is this backwards?

"The billions of dollars sent out of our country could be spent in America on such services as: healthcare, education, infrastructure, the elderly, elimination of the deficit, the building up of a surplus, aiding failing cities, providing for the less fortunate, providing opportunities for the willing. The citizens would expend their energy and expertise to revitalize America and put it in a better place." he states.

Then as an added note, Al says, "There are countries in the Middle East where the leaders and governments provide free housing, medical care and education for most of their citizens due to the amount of oil they have (read—money) thanks in large part to America. Therefore, many of their citizens spend their time doing little work and live the 'good life' because many of their services and needs are provided for by the government and others. A large part of their needed workers come from other countries, usually at low wages. The citizens spend their money on themselves, and, what is amazing, it seems that no other nation objects to it! Nobody expects them to give of themselves as America does. And, they get away with it! Why can they do it and we, America, cannot?"

Al continues, "Then, after the two years, and after we are in a very good place and situation concerning our expenditures and the care of our citizens, we can tell the world we can help again. We are not trying to remove ourselves forever from our destiny and goals; we are simply trying to get ourselves put back on solid ground so we can do what we want and need to do for Americans without harming ourselves."

Biljana then asks "What would happen, politically, to the other countries? Would some other power take over the smaller and poorer countries? Would the unjust leaders of some of those countries continue to smother their people to put them into an even worse place? Could those countries recover from the loss of aid during the two years?"

"Good questions," Al answers. "I am not sure I have answers, but I do have some observations."

Al then goes on. "Obviously, after the two years of self building, the United States would be in an excellent condition United deficit. Psychologically, we would feel better. Militarily, we could build up our forces and capability to have even greater confidence in our ability to protect ourselves. Furthermore, American individuals and companies would be in a better position, and in a better state of mind, to help others because their personal and individual situations would be secure."

He continues, "The other countries would then become more receptive and grateful to Americans giving to them. They will have had time to reconsider their stance in relation to their acceptance of us, in terms of recognition. Possibly, and hopefully, they would help themselves along with the American aid given to them, and use it properly. They would see that there are no two dollar bills; therefore, nothing is going right for them. They might even say thank you."

"Furthermore," he says, "I believe it is necessary to convince the other countries to help themselves more and more as time passes. When you think about it, some countries, specifically in the Middle East, that have received aid from America for decades to develop their resources (read—oil), show no inclination to take over the business of their respective countries to put them in a form that is better than an earlier time. They have developed their available resources to the point that almost the entire world depends on those resources. The leaders and individuals of those countries were earning more money than could be counted. They showed no proclivity to take over the reins of their governments in the manner which allowed them to gain such wealth. They continue to rely on American money, talent, supplies, etc., while not returning any favors. Maybe favors is the wrong word—maybe I should say obligations. And, on top of it all, these countries say disparaging things about America—but, only after they have taken it all. Unimaginable consequences!"

In the April 15, 2008, newspaper The Gazette, in Colorado Springs, Colorado, a letter to the editor written by Phil Kenney stated—"Iraq....we've given you enough blood and treasure, neither of which we can afford; its time you get off your butts and standup and defend the freedom we gave you..." (7).

8
WHAT IT MEANS

Time and time again, as they were lounging on the beach or walking down the street or working in their condo, Al and Biljana talked about this subject, and continued to get deeper into it. They dug back to what the motives of his parents, and Biljana herself, were, to relocate to America and what the processes were to become part of their new culture and environment.

Al related that his parents came here to become entrenched in the freedom and opportunities that they had heard and read about. Not necessarily that the streets were paved with gold, but that they could develop whatever they could figure out for themselves. They arrived willing to do whatever was necessary to become American citizens, to become members of a society that would accept them, to give of themselves to such a cause. After all, they knew nothing but misery and discrimination and belittlement in the shtetl they left near Kiev in Russia.

They told him about the pride they developed in being allowed to grow as much as they could and in having the right to do the best they can. They mentioned that immediately upon arriving in Philadelphia, they were helped by private groups and associations, as well as family members, who had been here for years, not the government.

This was such a common scenario, that, all of those immigrants who came to America added to the fabric of the Country; and accepted America completely. There was no thought of trying to change it. After all, America was what they wanted—why would they change it?

Even with these humble beginnings, just as millions of others from all over the world, Al's parents' idea was to accept their decision and to become the very best they could—to be proud of their newly adopted country. Al's father was even drafted into the American Army for World War I and was sent to France where he was wounded. His wound became a symbol of pride for him throughout his life.

Al's Mother was so intent on continuing to learn about America, that, later in life she read President Harry S Truman's biography. Because of not having formal education, she took a long time to read the book—with pride.

These incidents became such a pride factor for them that they beamed every time there was talk about it. Al's parents were determined to become American citizens and true Americans no matter how long it took or how much work it would be. "And, as a result, I had opportunities handed to me." Al reckons.

Biljana's first experience after arriving in America intensified her desires. She had been hired as a waitress at a military Officer's Club in Washington, D.C., even though she didn't speak English. She would try to write the orders down to take to the kitchen, but would have trouble. The American boys at the table would write the order for her, and she would take it to the kitchen. Upon delivering the orders to the table, she didn't know which plate went to whom. So, being enterprising, she would put all of the plates on the table, and the boys would pick out their orders. Now, what ensued convinced her of her decision. The customers did not hold anything against her, and left her a very large tip. Biljana says that "the people in no other country would act like this." Her biggest impression of Americans is that they are so naturally embracing.

Biljana had the same pride as Al's parents. The difference was, she had made the decision for herself, by herself and was ready to take the responsibility to do what was necessary. She created the opportunities for herself because she could and had the ability. The end result was to be the same. And, she was successful. She did not burden the government, the system, or those who were helping her. She is today, very proud of her achievement.

President Teddy Roosevelt wrote: "In the first place we should insist that if the immigrant who comes here in good faith becomes an American and assimilates himself to us, he shall be treated on an exact equality with everyone else, for it is an outrage to discriminate against any such man because of creed, or birth place, or origin. But this is predicated upon the man's becoming in very fact an American, and nothing but an American…There can be no divided allegiance here."

Both Al and Biljana noticed that as they spoke about this history of themselves, the common thread was that they were to become an integral part of their government, culture and society, not to be separated from it. This did not mean that they would abandon their personal experiences. It was important to them to maintain the traditions, background, language, history that they knew about themselves and their families. However, this part was personal, not a requirement of their adopted country.

So, the experience in Mexico was beginning to teach Al and Biljana something about themselves as well as about how other people think—like the woman from Scotland, and, the young American people who were saying disparaging remarks about America and Americans.

To further the assimilation to America by others, Al and Biljana, while living in Mexico, were told by some Mexicans that they couldn't refer to themselves as "American" because the term did not only include those from the United States of America. They were told that they are "Estadounidenses." The theory is that since the peoples of Canada, North America, Central America and South America are all on the same continent, the term American defines them all. This was the first time that Al and Biljana ever heard of such a thing. Very disturbing! Where in the world did that concept come from?

"This begs some questions" Al notes. "Are the people of the United States of Mexico known as Mexicans or Americans? Should then the people of the United States of America be called United Statesians? After all, our country is the United States of America, so why are we not Americans? Why are the people from Canada called Canadians? Why are the people from Venezuela called Venezuelans? Somewhat confusing, wouldn't you say?"

Al and Biljana felt the backlash of being a foreigner in Mexico with an incident that occurred during their attempt to follow the laws and rules of immigration. When going to the local immigration office to fill out the required forms and adhere to the rules, they were given a rude awakening. By asking questions of a woman at the front desk, they were told to get help and the proper papers from a gentlemen who had a desk outside of the immigration office. He was not a government employee, but rather, an enterprising person in the business of providing what papers the government needs at that office. It turned out, they learned later on, that he was the husband of the woman at the front desk of the immigration office who told us to see him for the paperwork. Dutifully, Al and Biljana did as was suggested. After some time and work with the gentleman, and after paying the costs, the papers were filled out and then Al and Biljana returned to the immigration desk to wait their turn. The same immigration lady called them, reviewed the papers and said that there were not enough papers, not enough copies, and that some of the filled out papers were wrong. They had to return to the gentleman in the hall to do it again. This process happened three times. After the third time, the immigration lady stated to Al and Biljana, that "If the papers are not complete and proper, we can deport you within 10 days." What?

This idea of not having the complete information to submit, they found out as time passed, was common and annoying. It seemed that everywhere they went to present documentation to authorities and sometime other professionals, it was not enough. They had to make more copies, get additional information, provide more papers than was originally asked for. It seemed that everything was arbitrary—the original requests were vague in the number necessary, thereby creating an opportunity for capriciousness.

Biljana read some statistics in an American newspaper concerning newly naturalized American citizens. She noted that California had over 297,000 residents become U. S. citizens in year 2008. With 22 percent of all naturalized citizens nationwide coming from Mexico, it is obvious that, happily, many people are doing things the legal way. Just the way she did. Good news.

There were times when Al and Biljana felt that they were not accepted as local residents. They felt that because they were driving their automobile around with American license plates, and did not look Latino, they were open targets to be stopped by the police. They had heard that this happens on a regular basis, because, as rumor has it, the police do not stop them to give them a ticket, necessarily. The stop is to extort money for themselves at the expense of the "visitor." This type of event was not limited to the police. Al and Biljana learned how important it was to have money available for obtaining all types of documents, approvals, agreements, etc. Money is the glue that ties things together. This concept was foreign to Al's and Biljana's sensibilities and experience. Very difficult!

Now, Biljana reminded Al of their trip back to Colorado after the three years residency in Mexico, since the trip consisted of incidents that are worthy of note. The journey was undertaken with the knowledge that their Mexican experience will aid them in the traverse of Mexico. After all, they were simply to drive their large sports utility vehicle from Playa del Carmen all the way into Texas and then to Colorado—a trip of approximately 3,500 miles and up to five days of travel.

Biljana says to Al "Do you remember that within the very first fours hours of the trip we were interrupted by a telephone call from our banker in Playa del Carmen?

The banker, who knows us personally, told us that the bank check that we wrote to deposit money from another bank into our account is not acceptable because Al's signature does not exactly match what they have on file. And, would we come into the bank to write another check. We were told that the teller has the right to accept or not accept a signature, and obviously, did not accept this one!" What? Unbelievable!

"We then had to scramble, remember, based on the suggestion of the banker who said he would telephone the branch manager about the situation, to find the branch outlet of the same bank in the city of Chetumal, and drove all around the city to find it." Al responds. The meeting with the branch manager was typically unresponsive and caused a lot of stress on them, but by writing another check and verifying everything with our banker, all was finally taken care of. "However," Biljana reminds, "the process took several hours to finalize and ruined our planned schedule for an overnight stay."

It must be stated here that all of the suggestions and comments made about traveling in Mexico by car tell us that one should not travel at night. The fact of possible "bandidos" stopping a car is a real concern. The fact that the roads are narrow and not always in good condition provide fodder for being concerned about potholes and poor conditions, and 'topes"—speed bumps. That people and animals are likely to be on the roads is also a fact. "And, to top it all off," Al says, "the road signs, or lack thereof, leave a lot to be desired."

In Mexico, crossing the line from one State to another can be a major undertaking. The federal army is stationed at every crossing and has the right to stop any vehicle to ask questions, to check papers and to search the vehicle. Sometimes the local police augment the army staff in these endeavors. Sometimes they simply wave you through. But, with Al and Biljana driving a foreign vehicle, with American license plates, and not looking like Latinos, Al says "We were easy targets for investigation." They had been instructed by others to be aware that most often an offer of some money was in order. They learned that 200 pesos (about $20 US) was appropriate. And, it turned out to be correct. As a side note, they were told that sometimes a Playboy magazine did the same thing. So, for Al and Biljana once again, the uncertainty of living a normal existence raised its head.

What made this part of the trip even more worrisome was the fact that as Al and Biljana traveled from the State of Quintana Roo into the State of Yucatan after the first night in a miserable hotel, they learned that there had been murders in Merida, the capital city of Yucatan. What was significant about this was that the murders were by the local drug cartel and that seven people had been decapitated. This impacted their attempt to cross the border into Yucatan because a search for the killers was on in full earnest.

Also, on the day before Al and Biljana left for their trip back to the United States, it so happened that, due to the local overt drug cartel method of expansion, the assistant police chief and his bodyguard were assassinated at the front door of his home. And, the mayor's daughter was abducted right about the same time. Is this some way to live? Does this strike the concept of fear into a person's psyche?

Similarly, as Al and Biljana traveled through the State of Nuevo Leon in the northern part of Mexico that borders Texas in the United States, they were concerned about the drug problems in that region. They had read and learned that the problem with murders, assassinations, kidnappings, and such were rampant in that particular State, and they simply wanted to drive all the way through the State during the day only. "Let's just get across the border" Biljana exhorts Al.

As they were driving and getting close to the border, with some sense of relief, their vehicle was once again noticed by the local police. So, they were pulled over within two miles of the port of entry. The policeman told Al that he was speeding, which was untrue, and extracted 200 pesos, which was the amount he requested.

Now Al says to Biljana, "The fact that we were so close to the border, I felt that the easiest thing to do was to simply pay the money, get him off our backs, get on our way, and cross into Texas and be safe."

9
WHAT IS EXPECTED

Al's parents and family and Biljana never gave a thought about what language they should speak. They knew that English was the language of their adopted country, so they learned English. They knew that since English was the spoken language of their adopted country, that they should not, and would not, ever require anyone to speak their native tongue. They knew that it was acceptable to speak their own language to whomever they wish, whenever they wish with no recriminations. If the other persons did not understand, then it was a personal thing. No mention of multiple language requirements. After all, they said, they are now in America!

They were told that they had laws and rules to follow, just as natural born Americans do. They were told that there is a legal process to remain in America to be a lawful immigrant, that they have to be lawfully employed, what they had to do to retain their lawful status and what was necessary to become an American citizen. "And, you know what," Biljana says to Al, "We followed the laws without question and without asking for any favors." They filled out the papers, reported to authorities according to the law and waited for their turn to raise their right hands to become true American Citizens.

The pride factor for them was enormous! What a wonderful event! What a personal accomplishment! Al's father Philip (Pinchus) would often exclaim "I just love America!" Biljana would say "Don't you love America?" It would be easy and normal to hear the reverberations of these same statements and sentiments throughout America throughout time.

So, what went wrong?

Once again, thoughts about this entered their minds while they were walking on the beach, enjoying the weather and ocean. "What happened?" they would remark. "How did our wonderful experiences change to what we hear today from others? How did things get so different? What prompted this opposite thinking?"

"Whoa, how can we even begin to get this straight in our own minds, let alone to get all Americans to recognize these facts and thoughts?" they remark to each other.

They knew that in earlier times and eras, there were political individuals in the world whose ideas included a desire to dominate the entire world. They had even lived through such events—Al during World War II, Biljana just after World War II and during the war in Bosnia. It was during those times that it was necessary to not only rid the world of such monsters and despots, but to prevent those tyrants from ever invading and taking over other countries to continue their rampages. They understood that those fiendish leaders would stop at nothing to gain their unnatural and egotistical desires to rule the entire world.

It was due to this awful reasoning by those rulers that the United States was willing and able to help other countries from being run over and dominated by those maniacs. So, the United States would agree to be the primary factor in repelling those invasions. In fact, some of the countries asked for, and in some cases, demanded, help from America to protect them from the maniacs. Basically, therefore, there existed during those times, a common enemy. Not only of specific countries, but to mankind in general. World dominance indeed! Inferior peoples indeed! The United States and all Americans, along with other reasonable countries, joined in the fight.

And, "Guess what?" Al says. "Those fanatics were all defeated!" It then came to the point that other countries expected, and demanded, America to help them in times of trouble. Bosnia, for example, was waiting for America to help during its war of independence from Yugoslavia, during the years from 1992 to 1995, when it finally asked for help. America responded and provided aid.

This means, Al and Biljana say to each other, that since at this point in time, there seems to no longer be a common enemy, amongst all nations, bent on changing the entire world for its personal political benefit, "We, America, do not have to be the world's police force any longer."

Although there remain hotspots in the world today where conflicts of ideologies still exist, the basic political world is better off and more aware today than in earlier times. With modern communication, more advanced technology to scrutinize possible threats, more history to review, more education, fewer megalomaniacs, it is possible to keep quarrels and differences isolated to prevent their spread.

10
SCENARIOS

Well, as time progressed, and discussions continued between Al and Biljana, the subject turned to what this is all about.

The talks revolved around what possibilities may exist in order to help America. A preface to the solution that evolved in their thinking had to be determined, in light of the direction their thoughts were heading. So, Al suggests a sort of isolationism. "Now," Al says, "various forms of isolationism have been considered in the past by people a lot smarter and experienced than I. Through that, I am aware of what the implications are. For our discussions, I will intentionally put aside those obvious implications."

He knew that Americans and the American economy were dependent upon foreign trade. He knew that farmers needed to sell some of their production to other countries. He knew that automobile makers depended upon sales in other countries. And, so on. He also understood that it is necessary for American companies and businesses to utilize what other countries have to offer in terms of expertise, products and talents.

But, in order to act like a scientist in this case, in order to put forth a premise, in order to think outside the box, Al and Biljana elected to ignore the obvious implications of the notion of isolationism. "How else can we think more clearly?" No obvious hurdles to begin the thought process.

Thus, it is time for us, America, to take care of ourselves for a while. There is no imminent threat of takeover, by some idiot leader, of the whole world. No individual, nor government, is making overtures to become the only and ruling society in the world.

"We can spend our own resources to repair our country at this time so that all of our citizens are in a good place with good and honest thoughts and ideas. Something of which to be proud. Something about which to brag. Something that will get into our souls and stay with strong convictions." Biljana says to Al. Al nods in agreement.

Al and Biljana's thoughts and discussions then turned to, in light of all they had figured out, what to do about the present day situation with illegal immigrants, and the migration to America of impoverished people from around the world.

"Big problem." Al says. "No easy solution, somebody will be angry at any suggestion."

Since they had been talking about how they got where they are (on a beach) and the way that it had been accomplished, they deduced something important. "Why should it be different for somebody today, than it was for others at an earlier time? America is still the same with the same ideals." After all, the goal is the same— to take advantage of the opportunities afforded in America.

So, the conclusion for them was that illegals should become legal so that they are not a burden on legal and tax paying citizens, and so that they pay their fair share of taxes to run the government. That way, there is no conflict, no repercussions and no arguments. If this means that some costs of goods and services will have to increase, so be it. The market place in America is a very real indicator of the way things should be. Whatever the economic implications are, they are.

If it means that some people will be inconvenienced, so be it. Al's parents and Biljana herself did not look at what they had to do as an inconvenience, but as an opportunity. If the illegals had done things the proper way to begin with, there would be no inconvenience, just safety and clarity.

After all, Al and Biljana had to comply with the rules of law, the cultural requirements as well as show respect in order to live in Mexico, which they did willingly. In fact, Al and Biljana signed up at a local school that taught Spanish to foreign speaking people. Even though they could have easily continued in this international community without a good knowledge of the local language, they decided that they should learn Spanish out of respect to their personal situation.

President James Madison said, "America was indebted to immigration for her settlement and prosperity. That part of America which had encouraged them most had advanced most rapidly in population, agriculture and the arts."

If individuals that emigrate to the United States wish to remain in their little private worlds with no regard to the greater picture, so be it. It is perfectly acceptable in America to have these enclaves of other cultures throughout America with little contact with the rest of the country—nothing wrong with that. It reinforces the premise that America is called "The World's Melting Pot." It still affords every individual the right to do as he pleases. Just so long as it is done in a lawful manner. After all, America is a country of laws.

The key to this is the phrase "little private worlds," as Al and Biljana see it. This implies that there is no discontent within the private worlds so as to force the country to bend to their ways and ideas.

America is still America. They knew that they could contribute to what America stands for and that it was not necessary to change anything.

11
CAN THINGS CHANGE?

In continuing their discussions and thoughts, Al and Biljana kept trying to dig deeper. Another thought that came to them had to do with a basic nature of Man. Since Man was given a developed brain along with a conscience, it implies that Man can create his own individual thoughts and actions. Therefore, it seemed to Al and Biljana, so long as there are two humans on this earth, there would be disagreement. This is because each has his own ideas. Now, it is up to these two humans to determine if the disagreement is to be simply a philosophical difference, or worse, conflict. After all, with the great variety of thought patterns amongst human individuals, it is inevitable that one would want to be the leader, and the other, not a leader, but not necessarily a follower.

President James Madison said, "As long as the reason of man continues fallible, and he is at liberty to exercise it, different opinions will be formed."

So, how do we integrate the need for disagreement with the need to cooperate? Whoa! Another significant question! How is this answered, or is there an answer?

Al had some basic thoughts about this some time ago. Now, it seemed a good time to develop them. A sort of philosophy that Al had created for himself was due to a single statement that was made in a class by a professor he had at his University. To paraphrase the statement, Al states "Life is a series of compromises." Seems appropriate now.

"You see," he says, "people compromise all the time on a daily basis. They simply do not realize it. For instance, if the restaurant does not have pickles, you opt for the available tomatoes. Or, if the shirt color is not red, you allow yourself to select the pink shirt. Or, if the computer disks come in packages of 100 instead of 50, you take the 100."

"Now," he continues, "what difference does it make? By selecting the tomatoes, was there any less enjoyment of the meal? By taking the pink shirt, did you look worse off? By buying the 100 disks, did you lose anything? Is your life any different? Did you change the world? Are you unhappier than before? Are you going to punish someone or something because of these compromises? Is it necessary to become angry or vengeful? Now, why can't this concept be advanced in all contexts, including government and foreign affairs? Is there really a difference?"

After analyzing what he was thinking about this idea, Al concludes, "Baloney, it makes no difference! All is the same as before! Therefore, it is good."

The problem is, of course, how do you get everybody to see this. After all, not all individuals think along similar lines—that is why indeed, we are individuals. How does a person with an "A" personality (impatient, time-conscious, highly competitive, ambitious) for instance, handle a situation that does not allow him to be aggresive? How can someone who is used to getting his way accept such a proposal? How does a country along with its leaders see the value in such a philosophy?

Another idea, as discussed between Al and Biljana, centered on the basic tenet of a contract. A contract, written or oral, presumes consideration on both sides of the contract—both parties will get something for giving something. Typically, one party offers a product or service and the other party provides payment in some form. This is consideration.

So, it seems that if compromises could be established, each party will still receive consideration. "If each party still receives basically what is asked for, then would not the contract be a positive transaction?" Biljana asks. If one side of the contract is unreasonable in its demands, then the contract becomes negative. She continues, "This accomplishes nothing and can contribute to conflict. In fact, it can nullify the transaction."

How does all of this relate to the original thinking of Al and Biljana? Does any of this make sense? Can it be put into practice?

A case in point, as considered by Al and Biljana, is the Middle East. From their limited knowledge of the situation, it seems that one party (The Palestinians) is unrelenting in its demand for the elimination of the State of Israel in order to have peace in the region with its own homeland. The other party (The Israelis) seem to be more willing to compromise for a peaceful settlement of the differences—offering to return the area taken during the 1967 war, which the Palestinians desire, and by releasing some prisoners of war, in order to maintain its security and safety. With this scenario, a contract cannot be valid—there is no consideration on both sides.

"Wouldn't both sides win if there was some compromise?" Al asks. "The Palestinians would have the land they want, and, the Israelis would have security and peace."

Seems like a logical conclusion to this situation. "One that would, or should, make both sides happy," Biljana remarks. And, it seems also, that America is working hard, and has worked continuously, to affect this compromise.

"However," Biljana says, "neither of the two sides acknowledges what America is doing. They just will not accept the fact that we are helping politically, monetarily, socially, to create normality in the region. They just take what we give." Does this mean that we should suspend our efforts and let them take care of it themselves? Al says, "Won't work. Recognizing that there are differences that are perpetuated by their own leaders, compromises seem to be out of the question. It is an all or nothing situation. Bad Karma."

This state of affairs will remain as is—a stalemate—so long as only one side of the contract is not willing to give even a little, while the other side does give a little or a lot.

This Palestinian/Israeli conflict is not an isolated scenario at this point in time. "Think about Serbia/Kosovo, Northern Ireland/Ireland, Pakistan/India, China/Tibet, Chechnya/Russia, to mention a few." Biljana states. "Not everybody in those areas, as well as others, seems to be willing to compromise to allow civility amongst peoples."

"Wow!" Al reflects, "This begs a question. Why do we hear nothing about conflicts in such places as Greenland, Iceland, Australia, Canada, Sweden, Mongolia, Samoa, Denmark, Holland, Ghana, Fiji, Madagascar, and others? Why is it always the same countries that fight?"

As time went on, Al and Biljana began to philosophize about other areas of concern. These areas took shape as they thought about America itself. "What could be accomplished in America by taking this step of a sort of isolationism? What would be changed in America to make this country even better, more humane, more accountable, more true to itself? Without harming itself, how would the individuals and citizens of America take to these steps? Would they be able to see and recognize the good that this all would appear to do?" asks Biljana.

"You sure do ask good and hard questions!" remarks Al, as he tries to conjure up some instances that would give answers.

"Let's see," Al begins. He starts to list some problem areas that should be fixed and for which he knew there have been innumerable attempts at repairing. Hard!

Al starts, "How about these? The welfare program, the healthcare problem, various aid programs to deserving Americans, equal and good education systems, elimination of quota-driven equal opportunity programs, priority systems to American made products and services. Wow! Just thinking about the many areas that need help is staggering. All the more reason to consider fixing them. All the more reason to tell the world we need the time to do our work on ourselves. Maybe one task at a time."

"Now, wait a minute," Biljana jumps in, "Do you think this is possible? I mean, the task you have mentioned is enormous. When dealing with so many people on so many issues and levels, do you really believe it can be done? Do you truly think that the career politicians will go along with this radical of an idea?"

"Well, my dear," Al says, "you have hit on a very real subject here that is part of this overall thinking. The phrase 'career politician' is a major stumbling block. These political leaders, at every level of government, actually do get in the way. Most of them seem to be much more concerned about the next election for themselves, than the fulfillment of the original charge given them by the electorate. Remember how many times I have stated that the original intent by Thomas Jefferson, a founding Father and third President of the United States, was that there should be no career politicians allowed. He also said that every fifteen years or so, there should be a minor political revolution so that America could rid itself of those elements of government that would become stale, unworkable and no good for America, and new and evolved ideas and methods could be installed and initiated. Is it time? Is it past time?"

12
SCARY THOUGHTS

"So," Biljana muses while having coffee one afternoon in their favorite place, Ah Cacao, sitting with other people and talking about different things, "this could bring up some more ideas. In fact, I have one." Al, of course, asks "Yes?"

"I have realized that there are a lot of Americans that cannot decide what they are; Americans, something else, or a combination." She begins to elaborate on the comment. "I don't understand why it is necessary for some people to refer to themselves as 'such and such—American'. Even the government has gone overboard in trying to be so politically correct that it has added to its questionnaires and applications boxes to be checked as to whether or not someone is "So and So—American." Not right. Even reversing the designations to read "American—So and So" would not be right. Possibly more politically correct, but not proper. In fact, hyphenating names tends to isolate peoples, not integrate." Heritage is important, it is just not necessary for it to be out in the open, to all people all the time.

Biljana expands her thought, "When people emigrate, the first generation of the family most often is referred to by the country of their birth. Their children, however, are of the country in which they were born. Other countries don't need this lengthy explanation of one's heritage, or, in today's terms, 'political correctness', why do we?."

Al grew up in a small town at the edge of the ocean in New York. The population of the town was comprised of people of all socio-economic levels from many parts of the world. There were Italians, Russians, Israelis, Poles, Chinese, Arabs, Germans, Irish, as well as people from around the Country. "Never once," Al says, "can I recall any group attempting to make changes to the methods and means by which America is governed. They all did what was legally expected of them and did not think of bending America to their ways. Also, some did live their lives the way they wished, with their own traditions and customs, but only within their own groups, bothering no one." He is sure there still is a large number of communities throughout the United States with the same scenario. Why is it different today? Did something happen in the span of years since he was a youngster?

Al and Biljana's daughter lives in California. She described a recent incident that happened to her in a local supermarket. She was at the check out register while the checker was speaking Spanish to the lady in front of her. A woman behind their daughter asked a question in Spanish directed at their daughter and was surprised that their daughter did not understand. The woman asked, in English, if she spoke Spanish, and the reply was "No.." The woman then exclaimed, "Well, you should!" Now, come on, is this right? Doesn't this type of attitude separate Americans?

Aren't we supposed to be united—the United States of America?

To consider oneself, in the public venues, African-

American, Hispanic-American, Asian-American, Mexican-American, Eskimo-American, South Pacific-American, Arab-American, Native-American—is harmful to the identity and sanctity of being American. "We don't see on the government forms such designations as Norwegian-American, Namibian-American, European-American, Mongolian-American." Al responds. "These designations" he continues, "tend to discriminate in favor of one group to the exclusion of all others, to the detriment of all proud Americans."

As Al thought about it, and talked to Biljana, it became obvious that something was wrong with the definition of being "American." Since when is simply being "American" such a bad thing? Why is it so necessary to have to describe oneself as a particular type of American to be proud? Al says "This is not to say that being proud of one's heritage is not important. It is just that the primary citizenship and loyalty is American. And, to substantiate this travesty, the government has buckled to the whims of certain vocal individual groups to their benefit and to the exclusion of all others. Not right."

It appears that, since the government and the media are pushing this sentiment, that the younger people are following suit. "These designations," in their minds, "become the correct thing to say and perpetuate" says Al. Al and Biljana agree that this approach definitely hurts their beloved country. Shame!

"In order to be the 'Melting Pot of the world'," Al muses, "It is necessary to be of one mind as it concerns being American, as it concerns patriotism. The way things are at this time, it seems, we are in what is referred to as the 'Salad Bowl concept' in America. This is where, instead of being a homogenous society (Melting Pot) of one mind and body as Americans, we are individual elements (Salad Bowl) sitting side by side with no combined posture"

This is in opposition to the concepts and documents as created by the Founding Fathers. Those concepts are meant to provide a formula and a foundation for Americans to be of one mind and body. "I feel," Al says, "that Thomas Jefferson and Alexander Hamilton would be offended by the actions of today's population in this regard. They would abhor the term 'politically correct'."

"I just thought of something else" Al says. "I have not seen in any other country, nor have I heard, where the people of those countries identify themselves this way. They simply say Italian, Hungarian, Japanese, Australian, Colombian, when asked what their nationality is. Why do we have to be so so-called politically correct? Or, is it really being politically correct? I don't think so. In fact, when asked what they are, do Americans answer Hispanic-American, Japanese-American? Nope. It follows then, that we don't hear such designations as Asian-German, Hispanic-French, African-Czech, Mongolian-Danish, Haitian-Vietnamese. It is ludicrous."

Where did this concept of "politically correct" come from anyway? Is it due to politicians who determine that they need the vote of their constituents who are of certain backgrounds? Is it that they are willing to bend the rules and ways and traditions of America's basic tenets and precepts to their personal needs?

So, this is what probably happens: initially, the professional politician, in order to get the votes he craves, somehow obtains the information and ballots in languages other than English. Because of this, he is a hero to the people in his district and is voted into office. Now, if this scenario remains local and at the expense of the politician and his supporters, it could be an acceptable scenario. However, when this becomes a part of the American way across the Country, especially using tax dollars, then it is disrespectful, dishonest and disingenuous, and can be considered correct only for politicians, not all Americans. Biljana says, "I have an idea. If you can't read English, you can't vote. After all, without understanding what is on a ballot, you might vote for the person you don't want, or an idea or law that is against your wishes."

None of what was being said between them was meant to intimate that pride in one's heritage should be denied, or ignored. Al always tells of his Russian background with satisfaction and dignity. Biljana talks of how important her Yugoslavian upbringing is to her and her family. It is just, that officially, they are Americans. How come others don't get it? Isn't it simple?

Biljana's brother is a Swedish citizen through the naturalization process. He knows that if Swedes would refer to him as Bosnian-Swedish, he would be highly offended. He has lived in Sweden for many years as a Swede and contributes to and loves his country. Is there a difference here in concept?

At one time in Colorado, Al listened to a radio talk show. The program's moderator was decidedly conservative. He had a guest on the air who had written a book after conducting focus groups and after taking polls, on various subjects. One of the themes of the book had to do with the demonstrable focus of attention given to America. The people who were interviewed were all Americans born of Mexican extraction. They all lived in America and were educated and employed in America. A question was asked of them—"If a war were to develop between America and Mexico, which side would you be on?" The answer by the people in the group was unanimously Mexico. "Now," Al says, "that is an impossible and unacceptable answer. How in the world do these American born citizens consider themselves something other than American? How do they reason that their loyalty goes to the other side, or anywhere other than America?" (8).

"We hear also" says Biljana, "that the extremist Muslims, or Islamists, have the same attitude. I hear people say that the Quran (Koran) talks about Jihad (translates to 'struggle' which apparently has deteriorated to mean a noble and holy war to eliminate all infidels -non-believers—or force them to convert to Islam). This group of people therefore puts America in a lower position and open for destruction. Some of these Islamists live in America."

On another pertinent reminder, it is important for all Americans to realize and remember that calling oneself "American" also transcends any political party. Only after accepting the principle that one is American, can it even be possible to align oneself with a political party. To simply put oneself out as a disciple of a particular political party, or as leaning to one side or another, without declaring the importance of being American, does no justice to the country. It is necessary to place the designation of American in the forefront in order to set oneself up as a member of a political party. In our political system, one can only decide to be a political party member after accepting being an American. "Too many diehard party members either forget this distinction, or ignore it. They think that a party is the be-all, end-all." Al says.

This is the same as saying there is only a single flavor of ice cream—chocolate. Similarly, Henry Ford is known to have stated, after he perfected the mass production of his automobiles that a buyer can have "any colour—so long as it's black."

In the era of the Founding Fathers, there were two parties created—the party known as the American Patriot Party (Whigs) and the party known as the Loyalists (Tories). The reason for the development of the parties was, at that time, to simply differentiate between those citizens who wished for a complete separation from England and the Crown (Whigs) and those who pushed to continue being a colony of the Crown (Loyalists). Straight forward and simple. Easy. How and why did it get so complicated?

Now, both Al and Biljana believe fervently that each person has the right to believe however he chooses. They realize that a large number of people put God in first position. This is acceptable. But, to not put America in the next position is not acceptable. "It is not right, nor is it a satisfactory scenario. Their priorities are wrong and they become a menace to the beauty and truth for which America stands," Biljana says.

"You know," Biljana says, "We can mention other aspects that are not only important, but are proof of that which America and its stable political system stand for. Even such seemingly mundane situations as crossing state borders without inspection or paper shuffling, gas station competition such that obtaining gasoline is not through a state owned monopoly, purchasing real estate by simply following the rules, having time limits on government agencies to provide answers and information requested, knowing that a government official will not ask for some unofficial payment in order for him to do his job, having the feeling of security and safety provided by the police and the armed services, are all part and parcel of America."

Further thought comes into their discussions while they continue on this train of thought, sipping a local beer on the beach. We read and hear about celebrities such as movies stars, athletes and headliners beating their chests about the terrible political, education and health conditions in which other peoples of other countries live. We see them offering their time, money and effort to aid these unfortunates for "the sake of mankind and humanity." Wonderful sentiment. Heavenly goal.

"It seems to me," Al says, "that if these same people were to apply these same sentiments and efforts to the country that allowed them to get where they are, that they would not only help humanity, but their own people as well. Giving back to those who helped them get where they are is vital." He continues, "It would be well for them to remember that there are Americans who are in dire straits. People all over our country need a helping hand with food, clothing, housing, medical care. In spite of what the world thinks, American streets are NOT paved with gold. We all have to work, worry, struggle, compromise, just as much as the rest of the world. We all have to remember that because we live in the type of society we have, we have the ability and opportunity to raise our standards. This is what we need to be proud of, and for which to fight. This is why all those American lives were lost in patriotic conflicts. We need also, to shout this to everybody in order to express our pride."

In fact, Biljana remembers, that during and after Hurricane Katrina, some people from other countries, and some people they knew in Mexico, talked about the fact that they did not know that there were American citizens that did not have much. They saw the devastation and horror on television, or read about it in their newspapers. They actually saw Americans without houses, without food, without medical care, without water. They couldn't believe it! Not everybody in America is rich?

It is necessary to become aware of some statistics about America's poor and homeless people: The third annual State Government Responses to the Food Assistance Gap in 2000 reports that the December, 2000 survey of all fifty States showed that 31 million Americans live in hunger or on the edge of hunger. It also said that New York City alone, reports 6,252 families are lodging nightly in city shelters.

A startling statistic concerning Americans, as reported by the National Law Center on Homelessness and Poverty, 2007, is that 3.5 million people experience homelessness in any given year. This is about 1% of the total population of America.

The U.S. Department of Housing and Urban Development

stated in March, 2008, that 53% of shelter users are single adult males, which constitutes 23% of U.S. citizens. Also, that 20% of the shelter users are children. The total number of shelter users per night across the country is more than 759,000 people.

Al noted that homeless people, shelter users, poor people, hungry people, are not relegated to any one particular area of the country. They are in many locations including California with 1.9 million people in severe poverty, Texas with 1.6 million people, and New York with 1.2 million people in the same circumstance. Other areas of concern include Wisconsin, Mississippi, Washington, D.C., Chicago, Cleveland, Detroit, Dallas, the Midwestern Rust Belt and, along the Mexican border. In fact, all of the States have some citizens below the poverty level, ranging from 7.3% in Maryland to 19.3% in New Mexico. The percentage of citizens below the poverty level in the Northeast part of the country, in year 2000, was 10.3%; in the Midwest was 9.5%; in the South was 12.5%; in the West was 11.9%. In year 2000, the poverty level was set at $21,065 per family, according to the U.S. Census Bureau.

Mark Rand, professor of social welfare at the University of Wisconsin, Madison, wrote "One in three Americans experience a full year of extreme poverty at some point in his or her adult life. An estimated 58% of Americans between the ages of 20 and 75 will spend at least a year in poverty. These estimates apply to non-immigrants. If illegal immigrants were factored in, the numbers would be worse."

The McClatchy Newspapers, in the Friday, February 23, 2007, edition, stated "With the exception of Mexico and Russia, the U.S. devotes the smallest portion of its gross domestic product to federal anti-poverty programs, and those programs are among the least effective at reducing poverty."

Wouldn't it be nice if we were to take some of our foreign aid budget and resolve this problem? Is this acceptable? Isn't it possible that by taking care of our country for two years, America will help its own to the point that these statistics will be overturned? At least, to some sort of acceptable level?

13
LET'S GET IT TOGETHER

From the book, *Revolutionary Characters,* by Gordon W. Wood (Alva O. Way University Professor at Brown University and Pulitzer Prize winner) states: "The United States was founded on a set of beliefs and not, as were other nations, on a common ethnicity, language, or religion. In order to establish our nationhood, we have to reaffirm and reinforce periodically the values of the men who declared independence from Great Britain and framed the Constitution.... Brilliance of their thought, the creativity of their politics, and the sheer magnitude of their achievement." (9)

We Americans need to remember that the reason we have paved streets, clean water, electricity, firemen, honest policemen, a public education system, libraries, efficient postal system, good healthcare, is because we have a government that utilizes the only political system ever invented that provides such freedom to its citizens without the personal desires of royalty, a dictator, a tyrant, a church or an emperor. This freedom additionally provides an atmosphere which allows the furtherance and the betterment of all, and each, of its citizens.

Encouragement is given to allow people to invent a better mousetrap. "Think of Henry Ford, Eli Whitney, Thomas Edison, Alexander Graham Bell, Jonas Salk, Bill Gates." Biljana mentions.

The Founding Fathers should be proud! The Founding Fathers could be proud! The Founding Fathers would be proud!

Gordon W. Wood also wrote, "Most Americans appear to believe that these revolutionary leaders constituted an incomparable generation of men who had a powerful and permanent impact on America's subsequent history. The founders appear even more marvelous than even those they emulated, the great legislators of classical antiquity, precisely because they are more real. They are not mythical characters but authentic historical figures about whom there exists a remarkable amount of historical evidence." (10) "Somehow for a brief moment ideas and power, intellectualism and politics came together—indeed were one with each other—in a way never again duplicated in American history. They were intellectuals without being alienated and political leaders without being obsessed with votes." (11) "As political leaders they constituted a peculiar sort of elite, a self-created aristocracy largely based on merit and talent that was unlike the hereditary nobility that ruled eighteenth century English society."

"Jefferson expressed his lifelong belief that the American Revolution would be 'the signal of arousing men to burst the chains under which monkish ignorance and superstition had persuaded them to bind themselves, and to assume the blessings and security of self-government.' He foresaw that eventually the whole world '(to some parts sooner, to others later, but finally all)' would follow the American lead. Sentiments like these became the source of America's messianic sense of obligation to promote the spread of freedom and democracy throughout the world." (12)

Also, American historian and author of textbooks and studies in history and political science, Charles A. Beard, wrote in 1912 "Never in the history of assemblies has there been a convention of men richer in political experience and in practical knowledge, or endowed with a profounder insight into the springs of human action and the intimate essence of government." (13)

Al remembered an essay he had heard about concerning America's early development of this new political system. He recounted to Biljana the integrity and ethics and dedication of some of the American Revolutionary War individuals, as cited by one Bob Aldrich.

Al relates and quotes to Biljana:

"Have you ever wondered what happened to the 56 men who signed the Declaration of Independence?

Five signers were captured by the British as traitors, and tortured before they died.

Twelve had their homes ransacked and burned.

Two lost their sons serving in the Revolutionary Army, another had two sons captured.

Nine of the 56 fought and died from wounds or hardships of the Revolutionary War. They signed and they pledged their lives, their fortunes, and their sacred honor. What kind of men were they?

Twenty-four were lawyers and jurists. Eleven were merchants, nine were farmers and large plantation owners; men of means, well educated. But they signed the Declaration of Independence knowing full well that the penalty would be death if they were captured.

Carter Braxton of Virginia, a wealthy planter and trader,

saw his ships swept from the seas by the British Navy. He sold his home and properties to pay his debts, and died in rags.

Thomas McKeam was so hounded by the British that he was forced to move his family almost constantly. He served in the Congress without pay, and his family was kept in hiding. His possessions were taken from him, and poverty was his reward.

Vandals or soldiers looted the properties of Dillery, Hall, Clymer, Walton, Gwinnett, Heyward, Ruttledge, and Middleton. At the battle of Yorktown, Thomas Nelson, Jr., noted that the British General Cornwallis had taken over the Nelson home for his headquarters. He quietly urged General George Washington to open fire. The home was destroyed, and Nelson died bankrupt.

Francis Lewis had his home and properties destroyed. The enemy jailed his wife, and she died within a few months.

John Hart was driven from his wife's bedside as she was dying. Their 13 children fled for their lives. His fields and his gristmill were laid to waste. For more than a year he lived in forests and caves, returning home to find his wife dead and his children vanished. A few weeks later he died from exhaustion and a broken heart.

Norris and Livingston suffered similar fates.

Such were the stories and sacrifices of the American Revolution. These were not wild eyed, rabble-rousing ruffians. They were soft-spoken men of means and education.

They had security, but they valued liberty more.

Standing tall, straight, and unwavering, they pledged:

'For the support of this declaration, with firm reliance on the protection of the divine providence, we mutually pledge to each other, our lives, our fortunes, and our sacred honor'."

They gave you and me a free and independent America. The history books never told you a lot of what happened in the Revolutionary War.

We didn't just fight the British. We were British subjects at that time and we fought our own government!"

Some of us take these liberties so much for granted—we shouldn't. Al says to Biljana "The sacrifices by those individuals should not be remembered only on the 4th of July. They should be always remembered, especially when it comes to being a proud American. After all, look what they gave us. Without them, we would probably be just a colonial outpost of some country. It is obvious that the American detractors of today do not realize what was accomplished by our history's ancestors." Biljana nods her head in assent.

"And," she continues, "let us not forget all of the men and women who have given their all subsequent to the Revolutionary War, to maintain and continue what we are talking about. They are all heroes and should be revered."

14

COMING TO AMERICA, SOMETIMES ILLEGALLY

Al says, "Why is it that so many people from so many countries try their hardest to come to America? We read and hear all the time about people who arrive legally and illegally, in comfort and in dire straits, with money and without anything, just to live in America—hoping to become Americans. Do we hear about Americans going to other countries to become citizens? Do we hear about Americans giving up their citizenship to live in other countries? I don't think so, though there are probably some rare instances."

In an editorial written in the Colorado Springs Gazette (Colorado) newspaper on July 3, 2008, the statement was made, "In America, each of us is free to seek our own dreams. But, we also must choose to serve a higher purpose, which is why it is called the American Dream. It's not Bobby's dream or Jane's dream. It's the American Dream".... "more than a melting pot, the United States serves as a safe haven of unity"…."We are the greatest nation on earth because we are one people united by a desire for freedom. We're the land of the free and the home of the brave…" (14).

Then, they both remembered a song that was written and sung by Neil Diamond. The song, "Coming to America" talks about people emigrating to America from all over the world. So, a thought comes to the two of them. Is there any other country in the world that has a song written about people escaping to that country? They both answer "I don't think so." This shows, once again, how important it is that America is the only drawing card for all people who wish to start a new life. This is further confirmation of the beautiful value of being in America, of being American.

Biljana reminds Al of the actual situation today in America as it relates to illegal immigrants. She related an incident, years ago, when Al needed some immediate medical attention in their home city. She drove him to the emergency room of a local hospital. It so happened that on that particular day, there were many people in the emergency room. Al had to wait four hours to be seen by a doctor, some of that time spent lying on the floor, in great pain, because there was no other place for him to lie down. What was of significance of this incident was that the majority of the people being treated seemed to be possibly illegal immigrants because we knew that city hospitals are required by law to treat any and every one. The thought that came to mind was that these possible illegals were using the emergency room as their doctor's normal office visit. They knew and heard about this situation of using the emergency rooms this way from medical personnel that worked in hospitals.

Many of them were there with, what seemed to be colds, sore throats and other minor ailments. Since they probably had no insurance, and since the government requires the hospitals to treat legal and illegal immigrants equally, this was the only opportunity they had to get treatment at no cost to them. Now, additionally, upon entering the hospital, Al had to wait in the waiting room while forms were filled out and insurance cards verified. Only after such confirmation, was he allowed into the emergency room to begin his additional waiting period. The question arises, "Did all of the legal and illegal immigrants get their treatment without such documentation and insurance?"

Now, Al and Biljana certainly were aware that not all of the patients in the hospital were illegal. Many of them were legitimately poor and could not afford any other medical treatment, but needed help. No problem. Giving aid is necessary; it's the American Way.

This brought up another, similar incident that occurred during their stay in Mexico. At one point, Biljana had to go to the emergency room of a local hospital. They treated her very well, did what they had to do, acted professionally. Except for one thing. In order for her to be released, she had to pay for the services rendered right there on the spot. Now, it is understood that payment was justified, and Biljana was willing to pay. But, in comparing this situation with the emergency situation with Al in America, the details show that immigrants in America are given better treatment than foreign inhabitants in Mexico. This scenario could easily be extended to other countries. Is this worthy of negative statements about America by Americans?

These events created some additional comments from both Al and Biljana. "How much was available to illegal immigrants in America? What do they get from the government? Do they receive more for paying nothing than legal immigrants and citizens who pay their taxes? Does the honest tax paying citizen receive the same consideration and facilities as the illegals?" Loaded question.

After deliberation, Al asks, "In what other country in the

world is the illegal immigrant received so easily? Where else in the world can an illegal receive health benefits, housing allowances, food stamps, clothing, a stipend, education, job opportunities, first choice over legal citizens, some safety from deportation, transportation, entertainment, police protection and, in some cases, all paperwork and signage in their own language? Who pays for these services? And, why do I have to press 1 on the telephone to hear a message in English? Does any other country have this ridiculous degrading annoyance? "Biljana answers with the obvious, "Only in America."

It turns out also, in Al and Biljana's experience, that without having made substantial monetary investments in Mexico, and, without being capable of sustaining themselves with sources outside of Mexico, they would not have been welcome as residents in Mexico. This prompted them to remember the fact that Mexicans, and others, can come to America with no money and no investments, and yet are still received with open arms.

"In fact," Al says, "Mexico's immigration laws are much more stringent than America's, possibly the toughest on the continent! Mexico doesn't give much room for error." To illustrate this point, some of Mexico's points of law as spelled out in it's constitution under Le General de Poblacion (General Law on Population), include:

Foreigners are admitted into Mexico according to their possibilities of contributing to national progress (Article 32).

Immigration officials must ensure that immigrants will be useful elements for the country and that they have the necessary funds for their sustenance and for their dependents (Article 34).

Foreigners may be barred from the country if their presence upsets the equilibrium of the national demographics, when foreigners are deemed detrimental to economic or national interests, when they do not behave like good citizens in their own country, when they have broken Mexican laws and when they are not found to be physically or mentally healthy (Article 38).

Foreigners with fake immigration papers may be fined or imprisoned (Article 116).

Foreigners who are deported from Mexico and attempt to re-enter the country without authorization can be imprisoned for up to ten years (Article 118).

Foreigners who violate the terms of their visa may be sentenced to up to six years in prison (Articles 119,120 and 121). Foreigners who misrepresent the terms of their visa while in Mexico—such as working without a permit—can also be imprisoned.

A penalty of up to two years in prison and a fine of three hundred to five thousand pesos will be imposed on the foreigner who enters the country illegally (Article 123).

Foreigners with legal immigration problems may be deported from Mexico instead of imprisoned (Article 125).

Foreigners who attempt against national sovereignty or security will be deported (Article 126).

A Mexican who marries a foreigner with the sole objective of helping the foreigner live in the country is subject to up to five years in prison (Article 127).

The Mexican constitution also ensures that foreign visitors are banned from interfering in the country's internal politics.

Do other countries have similar stringent requirements?

Now, does this make our system right? Is it a requirement that Americans should deny their own citizens to make the illegals comfortable? Doesn't it make sense to take care of one's own before being available to others, especially illegals? What do individual families do? Why, even when flying on an airplane, the flight attendants instruct all passengers to put the oxygen mask on themselves before helping someone else!

Are these following statistics true? Al was told of interesting information reportedly from the Los Angeles Times newspaper:

1. 40% of all workers in L.A. County (L.A. County has 10.2 million people) are working for cash and not paying taxes. This is because they are predominantly illegal immigrants working without a green card.

2. 95% of warrants for murder in Los Angeles are for illegal aliens.

3. 75% of people on the most wanted list in Los Angeles are illegal aliens.

4. Over 2/3 of all births in Los Angeles County are to illegal alien Mexicans on Medi-Cal, whose births are paid for by taxpayers.

5. Nearly 35% of all inmates in California detention centers are Mexican nationals here illegally

6. Over 300,000 illegal aliens in Los Angeles County are living in garages.

7. The FBI reports half of all gang members in Los Angeles are most likely illegal aliens from south of the border.

8. Nearly 60% of all occupants of HUD properties are illegal.

9. 21 radio stations in L. A. are Spanish speaking.

10. In L.A. County, 5.1 million people speak English, 3.9 million speak Spanish.

11. Less than 2% of illegal aliens are picking our crops, but 29% are on welfare. Over 70% of the United States annual population growth (and over 90% of California, Florida, and New York) results from immigration.

"What do we make of all of this information and of these facts? Where do we go from here? How can we make any changes? Do we need to make changes?" Al asks. "Do we give this straightforward information to all Americans? How will they react to it?"

Mark Krikorian, author of "The New Case Against Immigration—Both Legal and Illegal," argues that although mass immigration once served our national interests, in today's America, it weakens our common identity, limits opportunities for upward mobility, threatens our security and sovereignty, strains resources for social programs and disrupts middle-class norms of behavior. (15).

Maybe, Al and Biljana start to consider, after all of this thinking, things should continue to be left alone and let things come as they may. Maybe all of this is right. Maybe this is simply the next step in the evolution of the United States. Maybe America's destiny is to change so drastically that it cannot be identified. Who would want this?

15
IS THERE SOMEONE
WHO CAN CREATE A SOLUTION?

Biljana ruminated about the financial situation and economy of America in 2009, which all ties together with the patriotism that seems to be foundering in our country at this time. She says, "How is it that in the days of the Founding Fathers, we were fortunate enough to have a relatively small group of individuals who were intelligent, reasonable, creative, brave, civic-minded, philosopher-statesmen, ready and willing to formulate a new political attitude to develop a new country? This new viewpoint by the Founders combined the thinking of many other earlier historical philosophers—Locke, Hume, Aristotle, Plato, Plutarch, Burke—who were capable of developing new thoughts based on human rights. I think those philosophers from history were not restrained by any political system because all they were doing was 'philosophizing', not trying to persuade their respective countries into changing their systems and could, therefore, open their minds. Our brave Founding Fathers showed they could manipulate and adapt that information for the benefit of a new country, and, freedom for all people, which is exactly what happened." Biljana then adds, "All of that was accomplished when the entire population of America was around 4,000,000 people and communication was primitive!"

During the French Revolution, Jacques Necker (1732-1804), France's statesman and reformist minister of finance for Louis XVI, stated: "There are men whose zeal ought not to be cooled: such are those who, being conscious that they are qualified for great things, have a noble thirst for glory; who, being impelled by the force of their genius, feel themselves too confined within the narrow limits of common occupations; and those, more especially who, being struck with the idea of the public good, meditate on it and make it the most important business of their lives. Proceed, you who, after silencing self-love, find your resemblance in this picture."

"Now," Biljana continues, "how is it that in today's time, with a population of almost 300 million people, we cannot locate at least one person who has similar capabilities as any one of the Founding Fathers; who can put together a method of controlling our situation? One politician, one political scientist, one philosopher, one theorist, one economist, one leader, who can combine all the good ingredients? Today, we have more history to review, more practiced experiments of political philosophies, more people, more education, better communication, and the freedom to think and speak." Come on, America, we can do better!

A thought comes to mind. Perhaps the fault lies with the concept of career politicians. Since they seemingly are concerned with their careers more than they are with the overall welfare of our nation, they simply get in the way of new ideas. In order to implement new ideas, assuming they have been studied and analyzed properly, the people in position and power need to know they can put the ideas into force. This apparently is not possible with people who are only concerned about their careers. This must be done by people who can not only see the benefit of change, but who are willing to put it all on the line, just like the Founding Fathers and others of that period.

Gordon W. Wood wrote, "Because public office was seen as an obligation, the founders often described it as an unhappy burden, as a wretched responsibility thrust upon them by the fact of their high social rank. We smile today when we hear politicians complaining about the burdens of public office, but precisely because the eighteenth century leaders were not professional politicians, such disavowals of public office and such periodic withdrawals from politics as they habitually made possessed a meaning that is difficult for us today to recapture." (16) "They did not conceive of politics as a profession and of officeholding (sic) as a career as politicians do today. Like Jefferson, they believed that 'in a virtuous government...public offices are what they should be, burthens (sic) to those appointed to them, which it would be wrong to decline, though foreseen to bring with them intense labor, and great private loss.'" (17) "Jefferson's suspicion was based on his fear of the unrepresentative character of the elected officials, that they were too apt to drift away from the virtuous people who had elected them." (18)

Alexander Hamilton, in a February 13, 1778 letter to New York State's first governor, George Clinton, stated that there was now "a degeneracy of representation in the great council of America (Congress)" the "effects of which we daily see and feel, that there is not as much wisdom in a certain body as there ought to be, and as the success of our affairs demands. Folly, caprice, a want of foresight, comprehension and dignity characterize the general tenor of their actions."

In late winter of 1778, Hamilton also said "America once had a representation (in Congress) that would do honor to any age or nation. The present falling off is very alarming and dangerous."

And, "it was time that men of weight" should "take the alarm" to purge Congress of "weak, foolish and unsteady hands" to avoid "the consequences of having a Congress despised at home and abroad." Appropriate today?

Hamilton also has written, "Whatever refined politicians may think, it is of great consequence to preserve a national character.... To violate its faith whenever it is the least inconvenient to keep it (will) unquestionably have an ill-effect upon foreign negotiations and tend to bring Government at home into contempt..."

Al exclaims to Biljana, "Wow! Did Alexander Hamilton have his stuff put together or what? Was he capable of seeing into the future to speak about today's situation?"

America pioneered the notion as well as the system, of offering aid to other peoples and other countries with no strings attached. The entire world has taken advantage of America's generosity and utilized this revolutionary way of thinking. Why don't the recipients come back to repay? Isn't it past time?

16

FOUNDING FATHER'S PERTINENT QUOTES

Thomas Jefferson quotes:

"If the present Congress errs in too much talking, how can it be otherwise in a body to which people send one hundred and fifty lawyers, whose trade it is to question everything, yield nothing, and talk by the hour?"

(Author's note). The Congress should be made up of people who are at the base of American thought and action. People who can listen to all sides of an argument and make decisions based upon their constituency and not personal agendas.

"My reading of history convinces me that most bad government results from too much government."

(Author's note). In today's time, there is more political history upon which to reflect. This should translate into the America government being able to use the information to benefit the population.

"The democracy will cease to exist when you take away

from those who are willing to work and give it to those who would not."

(Author's note). Is this philosophy one we need to worry about? Especially the giving to peoples outside of our borders. America does not get the respect it deserves.

"When a man assumes a public trust he should consider himself a public property."

(Author's note). Public officials need to maintain their charge by the citizenry to do the work that the citizens have given them. Personal gain by the officials is not a prerequisite for the office.

"Experience hath shewn, that even under the best forms of Government, those entrusted with power have, in time, and by slow operations, perverted it into tyranny."

(Author's note). We have all seen and read about examples of just such perversions. All the more reason to limit the terms of all public officials, elected or appointed. This will eliminate, or at least minimize, the temptation for personal gain.

"Every generation needs a new revolution."

(Author's note). The revolution referred to means a change in personnel and some direction. To eliminate that which is no longer viable or contemporary is to advance civilization. To add that which is favorable and correct to the present time is to provide the citizenry with better government.

Alexander Hamilton Quotes:

"A feeble executive implies a feeble execution of the government. A feeble execution is but another phrase for a bad execution; and a government ill executed, whatever may be its theory, must be, in practice, a bad government." Federalist Paper No. 70, 1788.

(Author's note). With our system of government, the people have a method of changing the way it works. Our system of checks and balances, our term limits of some offices and with our voting system, we can make changes. It may take time and effort, but the concept is in place and is legal.

"A fondness for power is implanted, in most men, and it is natural to abuse it, when acquired." The Farmer Refuted, February 23, 1775.

(Author's note). Our system of government allows for access to and observance of our officials by the citizenry as well as communication of their actions to the general public. We have the power, then, to make decisions and changes.

"Foreign influence is truly the Grecian horse to a republic. We cannot be too careful to exclude its influence." Pacificus No.6, July 17, 1793.

(Author's note). We have seen many times how pressure, persuasion and manipulation by other countries and their leaders have affected our Country, both good and bad. From the beginning of the creation of America, our citizens have been swayed by words, styles, designs, concepts, philosophies of other nations. Don't we have our own schemes, systems and modes?

"Government implies the poser of making laws. It is essential to the idea of a law, that it be attended with a sanction; or, in other words, a penalty or punishment for disobedience." Federalist Paper No. 15, 1787.

(Author's note). One of the differences between America and some other countries is that our legal and judicial system is based on laws and human rights that pertain to all citizens.

"I will venture to assert that no combination of designing men under heaven will be capable of making a government unpopular which is in its principles a wise and good one, and vigorous in it operations." Speech to the New York Ratifying Convention, June, 1788.

(Author's note). This should be a tenet by which the

government works. We have seen that some actions by various government individuals have harmed the legitimate place to which America belongs in the world.

John Adams Quotes:

"The United States of America have exhibited, perhaps, the first example of governments erected on the simple principles of nature; and if men are now sufficiently enlightened to disabuse themselves of artifice, imposture, hypocrisy, and superstition, they will consider this event as an era in their history....it will forever be acknowledged that these (American) governments were contrived merely by the use of reason and the senses."

(Author's note). We know by the experience and history of America that the basic tenets, rules, regulations and laws that the Founding Fathers created have shown that human rights, reason and a government by the people is successful. All citizens have rights that prior to such creation, did not have.

"Government is instituted for the common good; for the protection, safety, prosperity, and happiness of the people; and not for profit, honor, or private interest of any one man, family, or class of men; therefore, the people alone have an incontestable, unalienable, and indefeasible right to institute government, and to reform, alter, or totally change the same, when their protection, safety, prosperity, and happiness require it."

(Author's note). America has proven, through the years and with many challenges, that what exists as a government had indeed been for the common good of all of its citizens, as well as for those who emigrate.

"Children should be educated and instructed in the principles of freedom."

(Author's note). The civics classes at all levels of education should indeed be teaching what the Constitution stands for. Only with this continuous instruction can all people not only be aware of their inalienable rights, but also what they can do about it, if they wish, and, to stand up for it.

"...no good government but what is republican...the very definition of a republic is 'an empire of laws, and not of men'."

(Author's note). Using the concepts of the ancient philosophers, as the Founding Fathers did, proved to be what is instrumental in the success of America. Laws, not men, is the only method whereby citizens are treated properly. If men only were to create and enforce the laws, then personal prejudice would be the rule.

"There is danger from all men. The only maxim of a free government ought to be to trust no man living with power to endanger the public liberty."

(Author's note). America has had its share of government users and power brokers. But, with our system of voting and checks and balances, we can control power.

James Monroe Quotes:

"The best form of government is that which is most likely to prevent the greatest sum of evil."

(Author's note). In America, we can control those concepts and individuals to prevent utter chaos. We know that sometimes it takes time and effort by a few gallant people, but in the short and long runs, the best prevails.

"Never did a government commence under auspices so favorable, nor ever was success so complete. If we look to the history of other nations, ancient or modern, we find no example of a growth so rapid, so gigantic, of a people so prosperous and happy."

(Author's note). As history shows, including our own, America certainly is the happiest of circumstances. That is why the rest of the world is so intent on either migrating to our shores, or attempting to emulate us.

"In this great nation there is but one order, that of the people, whose power, by a peculiarly happy improvement of the representative principle, is transferred from them, without impairing in the slightest degree their sovereignty, to bodies of their own creation, and to persons elected by themselves, in the full extent necessary for the purposes of free, enlightened, and efficient government."

(Author's note). America has had, and will continue to have from time to time, circumstances that question the role of individual sovereignty as well as the effectiveness of its many representatives. However, due to the brilliance of the Founding Fathers and their documents, we have methods and means of controlling and/or changing such events.

James Madison Quotes:

"If men were angels, no government would be necessary."

"If Tyranny and Oppression come to this land, it will be in the guise of fighting a foreign enemy."

(Author's note). America needs to continue its vigilance in keeping most negative foreign ideals and aggression from our shores. We have been successful in this regard.

"It is a universal truth that the loss of liberty at home is to be charged to the provisions against danger, real or pretended, from abroad."

(Author's note). America and Americans are aware that in order to maintain its safety from outside interests, that a solid and modern military force is necessary. The Founding Fathers knew this and placed it in their documents. Today, we continue down that path, for as it is said "To prevent war, we must be prepared for war."

"It will be of little avail to the people that the laws are made by men of their own choice if the laws be so voluminous that they cannot be read, or so incoherent that they cannot be understood."

(Author's note). We have been told that the number of laws and the vocabulary used for the laws is indecipherable. The reasons for this include that each law must be so complete and so comprehensive that all factors of our free society are accounted for. As our history continues, laws constantly get re-interpreted to the present time. This is a consequence of a free society run by common man. However, it makes sense that there should be some sort of description that all citizens can understand of these laws to be able to conform to them.

"No nation could preserve its freedom in the midst of continual warfare."

"The essence of Government is power; and power, lodged as it must be in human hands, will ever be liable to abuse."

(Author's note). Because Man was created with a mind and a conscience, it is understood that differences between men will appear. Our system of government has the happy ability to prevent and/or eliminate abuses by the power of the individual citizen. America especially has taken the high road and understands that, even though power can be abused, has the capability of making changes for the better without chaos and turmoil.

"The means of defense against foreign danger historically have become the instruments of tyranny at home."

(Author's note). America and its practiced system of government has shown that any outside attempts to subvert the Country have not harmed the basic tenets of the American way. We continue to be strong and the world leader.

"The truth is that all men having power ought to be mistrusted."

(Author's note). It is necessary to constantly scrutinize the authority of those in power. It is the only way that the citizenry can control the government. We, here in America, have the laws and principles that allow it, based on the documents as created by the Founding Fathers.

17
INTEGRATION OF PHILOSOPHIES

These discussions between Al and Biljana began to set some thoughts of what has happened with all of this. They attempted to put things together.

Thomas Jefferson's notion of what America could be is to be remembered. Since he was a deep thinker and a very honorable man with profound honor, integrity and ideals, his idea contemplated the place that America needs to take in the world of nations. His idea was that America, and its government, should not be simply a reincarnation of previous successful nations or governments. To recreate the success of the ancient Egyptian, Greek and Roman, and similar, civilizations was not enough. To only get to that level was simply another attempt at that which eventually failed. Jefferson's ideal was to go above that, to be loftier, to reach a plane that not only includes the virtuous elements of those earlier civilizations, but to learn from their failures and go higher; a government that was human in nature; a noble government; a dignified government and society; a government of laws for all citizens, not of individual rule and whim.

Jefferson's design for America was that it should be agrarian in nature with minimal intrusion by government and a decentralized government. Each family, on the other hand, could be considered a democracy, or a republic in itself within the rules. The family would make its own decisions for its own good. The government would provide only those decisions having to do with what government is designed to do for the general citizenry—infrastructure, safety, security from invasion, protective military force, currency, laws, judicial process, international relations. In other words, the government maintains only that which keeps order amongst the citizens and its relations to other nations.

Alexander Hamilton's design for America, on the other hand, was that all of its citizens are to take advantage of that which is made available by everyone; that a centralized government provides its citizens with all of the progress made by others. The government does more for its people than the people may need. This way, one person's progress is available to all others.

Both Thomas Jefferson and Alexander Hamilton, indeed, all of the Founding Fathers, had a vision of a noble America, one that has faith in its own future prosperity and dignity, where fulfillment of one's own thoughts can be developed and realized, where a free market permits its citizens to develop their potential to any degree they wish, to value any and all things, to live unmolested, to have the luxury of legal discontent, and, even to fail without recrimination.

This is a quote from an unknown source: "The Constitution is in strong need of a strong people to uphold it. The Constitution is under attack, a usurpation of government officials, lawmakers, media and a growing number of ignorant people who know nothing about the foundations of their own country, and seem as though they could care less."

In the book "Alexander Hamilton, A Life" by William Sterne Randall, on page 387, it says "The Founding Fathers, including

Hamilton, did not believe that, besides providing creative dissent, political parties could provide support, especially in presenting innovations. Parties were seen as destructive forces." (19).

Gratefully, as Al and Biljana see it, in today's time, America is a combination of the two philosophies, Jefferson's and Hamilton's. Each family can do what it considers necessary for itself, within the law. And, everybody benefits from the endeavors of others, as they wish, within the law. "This is where American pride must take precedence," they say.

As they reflect upon their initial observations and revelations and ruminate about their findings, Al and Biljana have determined that in spite of all the negativity said about America, in spite of all the research done on their parts concerning questions of impropriety and possible misuse, in learning about others and how they justify their thinking, America is still the best in the world, has the best governmental system ever devised and is still the most free place on the planet.

"So," Al says to Biljana, "let us agree that all people of and in America—natural born, naturalized immigrants, other immigrants, those who speak English, those who do not speak English, those who are capable of accomplishment, those in need of aid—will see and recognize that America has been and continues to be at the forefront of civility, of progress, of understanding, of sharing, of giving and of responsibility. And, also to trust that we have given all Americans a realization and understanding of what the Founding Fathers, along with all of those who have sacrificed for the good of our country, have accomplished for each and every one of us and all those yet to come."

Al and Biljana have a fervent desire that other nations will understand the present situation that America is in, will give the deserved credit to America and Americans for their willingness to be the father figure of the world and will acknowledge America's many contributions to the world and its inhabitants.

We should all join together in an American patriotic challenge; let us all be a part of a solution. Steps which can help include: Can we each select a method to support American patriotism? Can we inspire others to support American Patriotism?

"You know," Biljana says, "we need to focus on preserving America as we know it, and as history has shown, because keeping America healthy benefits not only America, but all people who need our help and those who hope to get it."

Patriotism is good and positive for all of us. Everyone benefits from it because it breathes respect for the Country that gives us the opportunity to be all we can be. It is now crucial for all of us to do our part.

Al and Biljana's vision states, "When our grand children, and all our descendents, read our history, they should be proud that we took the high road (remember that it was Thomas Jefferson that looked to create America to be at the highest level of integrity and honor) to be part of a positive solution and that we hopefully awakened the consciousness of all American people. Then, and only then, will there be a well deserved posture of American patriotism. Then, maybe, other countries and peoples, will express gratitude for what America has done for them."

It has been said that America is not only a place—it is a nation, and, its people are not only residents—they are citizens. Perfect!

ACKNOWLEDGMENTS

It is important to us to recognize the many people who helped us along the way.

Those who offered advice, observations and comments include Al's brother Marty and cousins Milt, Les and Arthur, and our friends Howard Dutzi, Steve Wisoker, Gary Blackman, Rick Broome, Barb Ziek, Karen Nelson, Jim McMullan, Mitch Christiansen, Michael Strait, Marvin Strait, Mike Gilbreth, Dixie Gilbreth, Jacqueline Haag and Bishop Richard Hanifen.

We thank them all.

BIBLIOGRAPHY

1. Armed Liberal, The Atlantic Magazine, Winds of Change.net article, *Patriotism Rears Its Head Yet Again*, October 5, 2007.

2. *Colorado Springs Gazette*, newspaper, October 20, 2008, by H. Blaine Miller, in part.

3. Article by Franklin K. Van Zandt, U.S. Geological Survey